REVIVALS OF THE OLD TESTAMENT

REVIVALS
OF THE
OLD TESTAMENT

by
C. E. AUTREY
PROFESSOR OF EVANGELISM
SOUTHWESTERN THEOLOGICAL SEMINARY
Fort Worth, Texas

Author of "Basic Evangelism"

ZONDERVAN PUBLISHING HOUSE
GRAND RAPIDS   MICHIGAN

This printing — 1963

To   the memory
of
DR. C. E. MATTHEWS

FOREWORD

Christians all over the world are praying for revival. Evidence that these prayers are being answered is gratifying. Over against the predominantly materialistic philosophy of multitudes, the moral bankruptcy of the social *disorder*, the collapse of character in high places and the increasingly pagan population, there is substantial evidence that God is at work in the world.

Religious denominations whose leaders two decades ago were saying, "Revivalism is on the wane," are now enjoying a revival of revivalism. The conscious need for spiritual revival is not felt merely by churchmen. The call is coming from the scientist, the statesman, the educator, the businessman and college student. Urgency is the appeal of the optimist and the pessimist.

God has answered the repentant prayer of his people in the past. The refreshing rains of revival have fallen from heaven to bring new life to many a sin-scorched land. God will send revival.

God's people have often prepared for revival by prayerful study of the revivals of the past. This book is a vibrant history of the outstanding revivals of the Old Testament. The scholar-evangelist-author presents the book with the hope that it will be so used of God's Spirit.

Few contemporary writers are as eminently equipped to write such a book as Dr. C. E. Autrey. After a remarkably successful career as pastor, Dr. Autrey became secretary of evangelism in the Louisiana Baptist Convention. So clearly was the hand of God upon him and so unmistakably was he talented in this work that he was asked to join the staff of the Division of Evangelism of the Home Mission Board. No one has doubted the leadership of the Holy Spirit in the selection of Dr. Autrey to teach evangelism in Southwestern Seminary.

This book will provide preaching dynamic and resource for the pastor, evangelist and student. It will provide soul-winning motivation and power for the layman. Well documented Biblically and historically, this thrilling and accurate story of revivals from the ancient past will be used of the Holy Spirit to fan the flames of revival today.

LEÓNARD SANDERSON
Director

Division of Evangelism,
Home Mission Board of the
Southern Baptist Convention,
Dallas, Texas

CONTENTS

REVIVALS OF THE OLD TESTAMENT

REVIVAL

THE MEANING OF REVIVAL

Revival is a reanimating of those who already possess life. Revival in the strict sense of the word has to do with God's people. It revives spiritual life which is in a state of declension. Revival is an instrument of evangelism. Evangelism is a far broader term. Evangelism is confronting the unregenerate with the doctrine of salvation. Evangelism embraces the reviving of the dead Christians as well as offering salvation to the lost. The prime purpose of revival is to revive the saved. When the saved are revived, it results in the salvation of the lost. In the Old Testament, evangelism is confined to revival. There is little or no effort seen in the Old Testament to reach the nations for God. Revival is any special spiritual stirring which turns the people back to God.[1] It is characterized by fervor and repentance. Often in the Old Testament, these revival efforts would last but a day or a week, but the effects would endure for a generation or more. Circumstances determined the duration. The Goshen revival seemed to last but a brief time due to the hardships in the wilderness. It lasted long enough, however, to create a sense of human dignity and nurture a deathless desire for liberty. It consecrated the people to a supreme task and swept them clear through the gates of slavery and beyond the reach of their slave masters. It put the Dead Sea between the oppressors and themselves. It gave them a leader and freedom. It moved them toward the Promised Land. Every revival makes a definite contribution to the life and progress of God's people.

1. *Revival is a divine method of operation in human history.*[2] At certain intervals a spiritual awakening comes to given areas. People are shocked out of indifference into a deep conviction of the need of God. They feel that they are offensive to God and that a fundamental wrongness prevails within them. The burden of guilt brings a burning desire to escape the doom which they feel is imminent. They cast everything aside and give attention to the weighty urge. When this occurs, there comes a quickening of life. God imparts life — that is revival. While revival is primarily for the redeemed, it also results in the impartation of life to the sinner.[3]

Often these revivals are local and never spread beyond their area. The revival which fails to extend beyond its local area is frequently just as real as the revival which spreads with amazing rapidity through an entire nation or continent. There have been nation-wide revivals and continent-wide revivals, but there has never been a world-wide revival. This phenomenon is still a hope. Some generation may well see it. A universal study of the revivals of the Bible could be the instrument to prepare the earth for such an unprecedented event. Herein lies the reason for this particular study.

A few pastors, in preparation for revival in the local churches, have given a thorough study to the revivals of the past, beginning with revivals of the Old Testament. Each week for three months the pastor will take up one of the great revivals of the past. The revival will be studied in detail. The origin, progress, methods, personalities, and results of the revival will be pointed up. Each time the study has been followed by a period of prayer. The folk are led to call upon God to do for them what He has so gloriously done before for others. In every place where this method has been used, revival has broken out weeks before the study ended. It is one of the most effective methods of preparation ever used in local churches.

The earliest effort to teach evangelism in the colleges and seminaries of America was a study of the history of revivals.[4] It was the idea of the educators that the best way to develop evangelists and to promote revival was to study the revivals of the past, their laws, and the great personalities whom God used in these revivals. If a well-planned study of revivals has been used to promote revival in local churches, and if the same type of study generates the spirit of evangelism within the hearts of young preachers, it may also be used to stimulate revival around the world.

This brings us back to the major premise that revival is a divine operation in human history. The recurrence of revival is part of the operation of God. One of the basic laws of all progress is revival. Revival is not confined to religion.[5] It expresses itself in every sphere of life. We observe it in political science. One nation, then another, rises to prominence and power only to reach its climax, then fall back, and another replaces it in prominence and leadership. Turkey was as formidable in its day in the East as Russia is today. Its waters receded. France, under Napoleon, was the mighty power of the world; then Spain, then Britain, to multiply illustrations, but none of them are great powers today. Britain and France are great powers but not in the same sense that they once were. They may arise again to prominence; only time will tell. Each made its contribution to civilization in its mighty surge upward and outward.

Literature has had its golden years. These years witnessed renewed interest in literature and fiction. Such a period was witnessed in the days of Shakespeare. There also have been revivals of commerce and science. This present generation is in the midst of an unprecedented revival of science. Because of the present scientific revival, our civilization promises to reach unparalleled heights of achievement in transportation, medicine, industry, and many other fields.

Revival prevents stagnation.[6] Revival revitalizes life. All phases of life do not move forward at the same time. To wait for such a phenomenon would breed stagnation and would poison all of life. Without spiritual revival, religious progress would be imperceptible. Hope and inspiration will accomplish much more than mere struggle without either. Life does not remain at the same level.[7] This is true of the individual, the church, the community, and the whole nation. Today, a man may rejoice in God and flex his mental and spiritual muscles, feeling equal to combat with Satan himself. Tomorrow, the same man, caught in a wave of distress and disappointment, may cry out for help like a little child. One day Simon Peter took his sword and cut off the ear of the servant of the high priest. But soon thereafter he cursed and denied Christ before the accusations of a teen-age girl who accused him only of being a friend of Christ. The power of Christ rescued him. A few weeks later at Pentecost, he was swept by a mighty tide of divine power and ascended to unparalleled peaks of victory and spiritual revival.

We have all seen churches whose services were poorly attended, organizations inadequate, and where vision seemed dim, to say nothing of their lack of enthusiasm. We have seen revival waves move over these churches, and in a brief time they would be put to the task of providing room for all who came to the services. Tides of joy and enthusiasm characterized the whole church. The churches moved up and out because of spiritual refreshing from above.

2. *Revival is an instrument of spiritual revolution.* Christianity is a revolution. It was never intended by its Author to be anything else. This does not imply that Christianity is a constant state of overturning and uprooting. There are periods of consolidation and organization in the growth of every healthy movement. Christianity is divine life within individuals. When the proportions of the Christian drive and fervor become less than revolutionary, it ceases to capture the imagination and attention of the world. Vital Christianity fits perfectly into the framework of this hour of revolutionary ferment. Real revival will produce some excitement. Man is intellectual, volitional, and emo-

tional. True revival will affect the whole man, including
the emotions. Excesses are to be curbed at all costs, but
emotions are natural and imperative in revival. There must
be enough wholesome excitement to stimulate moral consciousness and neutralize the effects of degradation.[8] Men
never respond until they are moved. Knowledge of facts
never moves men. Statistics on the number of deaths and
distress caused annually by alcoholic beverage never con-
vert drunkards. Figures on the percentage of increase of
crime never change criminals. Men must be moved by the
convicting power of the Holy Spirit.

3. *Revival is a miracle.* It does come from God, but
man may promote revival. God sends the sunshine and
the rain. God made the fertile soil. These elements are
essential to a good corn crop, but man must till the soil
and work in the field or the harvest will never be realized.
The ear of corn, and even the stalk, are miracles, but the
seed must be planted and the fruit gathered. All great revivals are the refreshing showers from heaven, but if one
will take the trouble to study these spiritual phenomena, he
will find that, in every case, at least a few good and faithful
people prayed and longed for the heavenly winds to blow
upon them.

The evangelistic campaign or the protracted meeting
is of recent origin.[9] Many of the religious epochal events
of the Old Testament, which are truly revivals, would not
be recognized as such if they were compared to the modern
revival campaign. Revival has a wider usage than the protracted meeting found in the Bible and in history. The only
revival in the Old Testament which is similar to the modern
campaign was the post-captivity revival which took place
under the leadership of Nehemiah and Ezra. It was an
open-air meeting. A high wooden platform was erected in
one of the broad streets, and the Word of God was read
from the wooden platform and expounded to the people.
They were greatly moved by the exposition of the Word
of God.

Why Study Revivals of the Bible?

1. *To impart the spirit of revival is probably the greatest benefit to be received from a study of this nature.* This has already been mentioned in connection with the definition of revival. A study of revival creates a desire to see revival. Many things entered into the great Dundee revival in the nineteenth century, but a study of the revival at Kilsythe was the greatest contributing cause.[10] Revival spirit is a contagion. To tell about a great revival currently in progress, or to study about one in the past, seems to cause almost equal effect. The contagion may be caught even from cold print on musty pages of history. The smouldering fire leaps from the yellow page to the heart of the preacher and the audience. From there, it is transmitted to the cold, dead world. In this very way, Dundee became a veritable fire zone. Reports of revival at Northampton in Jonathan Edwards' church spread the flame to all of New England. Preachers and laymen would tell what they had seen and felt at Northampton. A study of the revivals of the Old Testament may generate revival spirit.

2. *A thorough knowledge of Old Testament revivals will give one an understanding of the methods used.* There is always a method of operation. Methods may vary with needs and ages, but methods are always present. In the revival under Moses, a tent was erected and the folk were urged to repair there for prayer. They were to pray directly to God. Personal religion was re-established. In the Mizpah Revival, Samuel called a great national assembly and confronted the leaders with the necessity of repentance. In the post-captivity awakening, open-air services were held. The Bible was read and expounded, and the people repented. The methods were always simple and were only instruments to bring the folk into contact with God. In no case were the methods used as an end within themselves. In no case did the leaders depend solely on methods. They recognized methods for what they were worth but remained aware that God was the source of spiritual refreshing. A study of Bible revivals gives us a vantage point which

guards against becoming confused by a great network of techniques which are to be our servants, rather than our masters.

3. *A study of revival acquaints one with the great personalities which were involved in them.* Some of these men were prophets, kings, teachers, priests, judges, and cabinet members of mighty empires. God may call a leader from any walk of life and imbue him with grace, judgment, insight, and power to lead the people in a mighty awakening. None of these great personalities were exactly alike. All were individuals. Most of them did not transcend at any point. They possessed the same fleshly desires that their contemporaries had, but all of them were completely possessed by a great idea and dedicated to a cause. Each one believed in a personal, living God and had a sense of destiny. Each had an indomitable courage and would not be detoured by pressures from without and fears from within.

It is possible to so study the lives of these great personalities that one may feel the spirit and atmosphere in which they lived. He may know them as well as he does his contemporaries. He may become familiar with their hardships, trials, and tears, and live over again their glorious triumphs and achievements. The great manifestations of power poured out upon the ministry of these men may become one's meat and drink. Close and wise association with the history of these men may breed vision within one that will equip him to be a similar instrument for revival in God's hand. If nothing else, it will affect the thinking of the student and "as a man thinketh in his heart, so is he." It is impossible to think and walk through the pages of Holy Writ with Elijah, Hezekiah, and Ezra and not feel the lift of their wholesome, personal lives.

4. *It prepares one to expect and accept revival when it comes.* When we understand the origin of revivals, the place of God's people in revival, and seek to meet the requirements, then we may pray earnestly, expecting refreshing from heaven. A knowledge of Old Testament revivals, as well as revivals of history, will prepare one to accept

revival when it comes. When our knowledge of past revivals is adequate, we will realize that no two revivals ever followed the same pattern. Preconceived ideas of what a revival must be like will be removed, making it possible to accept revival when it comes. Often, revivals have been rejected by our leaders because they took on a form which was new and unexpected.

FEATURES OF REVIVALS

1. *Spiritual degradation and despair precede revival.*[11] Before the first Old Testament revival, Egyptian bondage had become unbearable. The Hebrews were oppressed beyond description. They were literally enslaved (Exod. 1:11-14). Pharaoh used them to build great cities, such at Pithom and Raamses. The Egyptians increased their burdens and killed their newborn babes (Exod. 1:16). The distress was sore. Such conditions generally lead to moral and spiritual degeneracy. In this case, it prompted the oppressed to cry unto God for help. A great return to God took place which gave the enslaved a force of character and determination sufficient to undertake what on the surface seemed impossible.

Spiritual chaos preceded the revival at Jerusalem under Hezekiah. They left the commandments of the Lord, making molten images and bowing down to them. They burned their children in the fire (II Kings 17:17). They resorted to divination (vs. 17). They lost their honor as a people and became a tributary to Assyria (17:3-6). Their homes, property, and sacred places were despoiled (II Kings 17:20). Spiritual blindness and moral impurities prevailed before the revival under Hezekiah. Distress was general, and pressures from without mounted in Jerusalem before the post-captivity revival. The people forsook the statutes of God. They no longer tithed (Neh. 13:12). They had forsaken the house of God. They ignored or abused the Sabbath. They had intermarried with other races (Neh. 13:23-27). The walls of the city were broken down, and they were scorned and pillaged by their neighbors. Degradation not

only characterized conditions before revivals in the Old
Testament, but it has been true of all revivals since. The
saddest picture of human degeneracy may be found in the
study of the days before Wesley in England, and the spiritual and moral destitution before the Reformation. James
Burns points out that preceding each revival there is a time
of hopelessness when a deep and dark lethargy settles upon
the people and there follows a turning away from the
church.[12] Outwardly, men perform religious duties with
marked regularity, but their hearts are not in it.

2. *A deep sense of sin and concern characterized each
revival.*[13] When revival deepens, men are convicted of sin.
In real revival it is never necessary to unduly urge and
press the people for decision. Sinners will seek the Lord.
When conviction gets so deep that men can neither eat nor
sleep, it will not be necessary to urge them. They will come
to the Lord. Certainly, we are to plead with men, but without conviction it will be futile. Pleading does not produce
conviction. The Holy Spirit works conviction. Evangelists
always call upon sinners to accept Christ, but in revivals
sinners beg Christ to accept them.[14] Sinners never do this
unless they realize their condition. A swimmer never cries
for help unless he is drowning. No sinner will call for rescue
unless he realizes that he is drowning. Revival brings men
face to face with their actual need. Revival awakens in the
church and the individual a sense of sin. Sinners see themselves as God sees them. Sin never becomes real to a sinner
until he views it through the living presence of God. Under
the divine pressure of the agony of sin, men confess their
sins. In certain foreign lands where the sense of sin is very
difficult to arouse, this agonizing conviction has prevailed
when revival breaks out. It is reported to be difficult to
arouse a sense of sin among the Chinese people, but in the
Shantung revival, men fell under the awful sense of guilt.

Revival always produces great concern in church members. Backslidden members are convicted of their failures,
and concern for the lost seizes the hearts of all. A mani-

fested concern for others is a sure sign that a Christian has
revival in his heart.

3. *A revival provides spiritual impetus for mighty ac-
complishments.* We know very little about the revival in
Goshen before the exodus, but it provided the impetus necessary to make it possible for several hundred thousand
slaves to throw off the yoke of their oppressors and brave
the perils of the wilderness. Like a mighty flood, it washed
away the cowardice and impotence of slavery and put
marching iron into their blood. The Colonial Revival of
America in the middle of the eighteenth century gave rise
to democracy in the United States.[15] The common people
were converted in large numbers in the revival. The new
birth of the common people helped them to realize their
worth. Baptists, Methodists, Presbyterians, and other evan-
gelicals who believed in religious liberty and separation of
church and state multiplied greatly during the revival. These
masses made themselves heard and their influence felt. As
a result, the growing idea of union of church and state was
abandoned, and religious liberty became a reality.[16] Revival
does more than wash away moral impurities and pull drunkards out of the ditch. It determines the type of government
under which we live and the polity of the churches. The
Colonial Revival established evangelical Christianity on the
North American continent. It removed the bonds of formal-
ity and set up a warm evangelistic form of worship. The
Colonial Revival was the determining factor in the formation
of the government of the young nation, as well as the religious coloring of the people.

The revival of the Reformation produced centers of
evangelical religion on the mainland and in the British Isles.
These centers were surrounded by formidable opposition.
Because of the opposition, thousands left Europe and the
British Isles and came to America that they might be free
to worship God as they pleased.[17] The intermittent waves
of the Reformation really laid the foundation for the migra-
tion to the New World. Without a sufficient religious impetus, the majority of the immigrants would never have sailed

to America. Just as the Hebrews left Egypt to find a place
where they could worship God as they desired, so North
America was settled for the same reason. The Samuel revival
led to the establishment of the nation. Revival builds force
of character and establishes national fortitude.

4. *Great leaders are discovered by revivals.*[18] The
Mount Carmel revival discovered the prophet of fire, Elijah.
Moses, Aaron, and Joshua stood out in the Exodus Revival.
The post-captivity revival evolved around Nehemiah, Ezra,
and Malachi. These were dedicated leaders in government,
religious teaching, and preaching. God endued them with
vision and ability to meet the needs of their particular hour.
Savonarola, a pleasure-loving son of a wealthy merchant,
became the instrument of awakening in God's hands in the
Middle Ages. The Reformation saw the greatest galaxy of
leaders and preachers of all time come to attention. Great
personalities like Martin Luther, John Calvin, Zwingli, John
Knox, and Bethasar Hubmaier burned and preached as no
other generation of spiritual giants. Revival often brings
to the front great leaders of marvelous ability.

5. *Great joy characterized the revivals.* After the revival in Goshen, the children of Israel sang for the first time
since their bondage (Exod. 15:1-21). Their conception of
God was put into poetry and they gave expression to it in
songs from the heart. They sang, "The LORD is my strength"
(Exod. 15:2). They sang of His power and excellency
(Exod. 15:6-8). They also declared in song His holiness
(Exod. 15:11). They sang of many other things. When
revival came to Jerusalem under Hezekiah, a new song was
born. "They sang praises with gladness" (II Chron. 29:30).
The Reformation was a time of gladness for the redeemed.
Luther, Zwingli, and most of the leaders were musicians
and made much of music to express their joy of soul.[19]

Singing expressed the soulful joy which accompanied
the Wesleyan revival. John Wesley wrote many new songs
and his brother, Charles, composed no less than six thousand
hymns. The English people lifted up their voices in song
as revival fires swept wide and deep.

6. *Prayer is one feature which is found in every great revival, whether it be local or continent-wide.* Moses alone with God in Midian prayed for the enslaved people. Before the great revival at Sinai, Moses prayed that God would not cast off Israel because they had sinned. He prayed, "Oh, this people have sinned a great sin . . . . Yet now, if thou wilt forgive their sin —; and if not, blot me, I pray thee, out of thy book which thou hast written" (Exod. 32:31-32). The revival actually began with the earnest, relentless prayers of Moses. Samuel prayed for his rebellious people and before the general assembly at Mizpeh he cried unto God for them (I Sam. 7:8). Elijah prayed at Mount Carmel, "Hear me, O LORD, hear me, that this people may know that thou art the LORD God" (I Kings 18:37). Before the revival of 1800 in America, the leaders organized for prayer until it became spontaneous.[20] Then revival came. Revivals have never come apart from prayer.

NEED FOR REVIVAL

1. *Revival could prevent theological stagnation.* Trends of the times tend to engulf us. We are pressed into certain molds by the spirit of the age. Great spiritual and moral dearth prevailed in England and America during the first thirty years of the eighteenth century.[21] Two things were largely responsible religiously for the spiritual decline in England. Deism had affected the theology of the preachers. Deism denied the revelations of the Old and New Testaments. It held that God could not reveal Himself to finite men. It taught that the voice of God in nature was a sufficient guide. The deistic system of thought believed in the existence of God but taught that it was impossible to contact Him.[22] This philosophy contaminated the theology of the preachers of England and America. It dried up pulpit vitality, and laymen were soon affected. By 1702, preaching in America had lost its glow.[23] Spiritual life became decadent and morals, even among preachers, were deplorable. When theology became stagnant, religious progress ended, and spiritual decay and moral ruin prevailed.

Vigorous Presbyterianism was killed in England during this same period by infiltration of unitarianism.[24] In less than fifty years of unitarian penetration, the doctrines of the great founders of Presbyterianism had been throttled and were heard no more. With the doctrine went the church. What a people believe, makes them. Doctrines which cut out the heart of evangelical Christianity will impair the churches and breed spiritual death and moral catastrophe. When the Hebrews, before Josiah's day, lost the Word of God, they lost their doctrines. With this loss went religious stamina and progress. They were in a sorry plight when the book of the law was discovered (II Kings 21:16).

The greatest contribution of revival today would be at the point of theological need. There is a variety of new emphases now, but many of them smack of compromise. They would bid for popular assent by a compromise of essential truth. It is fair to say that theology in America is more virile than anywhere else in the world. Christianity, in every generation or location where it seeks to win the assent of current culture by accommodating itself to the contemporary mind, is weak and unimpressive.[25] This does not mean that there is any merit in being unintelligible or outmoded. It simply implies that a firm stand for essential truth which burns with new vitality is the answer. Truth does not change, but language and thought forms constantly change. In our effort to remain in the orbit of the spirit of our age, we often, unawares, take liberties with the truth. These liberties ultimately lead to spiritual decline.

Higher criticism, especially source criticism, has its place, but form criticism tends to stagger the faith of the young preacher. It holds that the stories and miracles in the Gospels are largely made up of unrelated anecdotes and other bits of tradition.[26] Form criticism contends that most of the incidents in the life of Christ were stories which circulated orally among the people but were not really true. The resurrection of Christ, for example, is considered legendary. The critics say it is natural that tradition, which was passed on orally, should take on a fragmentary and unrelated character, such as that which they claim to be found in the Gospels.[27] Since each section of the material could be taken out of its context and still stand complete and self-explanatory is sure proof, they claim, that the stories were circulating legends which evolved around an extraordinary personality.

"Form criticism is an attempt to apply conclusions reached by students of folklore to the tradition of early Christianity preserved in the Gospels."[28] Dibelius and Bultmann are the recognized leaders in the field of form critcism. In the Gospels the stories and dialogues of Jesus are often associated with miracles, and they generally led to striking pronouncements by Jesus. Dibelius teaches that Jesus did not make these pronouncements, so capable of general application. He says that these pronouncements were added by preachers who related these incidents.[29] Bultmann goes even further and declares that the stories were invented to give setting and meaning to the pronouncements. These critics look on the miracles of Jesus as tales. The miracle-tale is generally more colorful than the paradigm. The miracle, however, is no more than a biographical anecdote. The higher critics contend further that some of the incidents and acts of Jesus were only myths. The story of the transfiguration is considered a myth.[30]

When the preacher loses faith in the Bible, he generally assumes the role of a critic with liberty to dissect it at will. When he becomes a critic rather than a proclaimer of the Word of God, his effectiveness becomes negligible. The Bible is the Word of God. The Holy Spirit guided men of old as they wrote the various books of the Bible. Revival could correct the spiritual stagnation generated by higher criticism. When men experience God and feel the presence of God, they will again believe His Word, and Christianity will become virile and aggressive.

2. *We need a revival today to stop the world from joining the church, and to multiply the number of true believers.* In the fifth chapter of Acts, the devil tried to poison the unity and spirit of unselfishness which prevailed in the

Early Church. He led Ananias and Sapphira to tell a lie, pretending to do and be something which they were not. When they lied to the Holy Spirit, they fell dead. The news of this strange phenomenon spread throughout the church and the entire community, and as a result, the world stopped joining the church. "And of the rest durst no man join himself to them" (Acts 5:13). This is a caution to loose evangelism which would seek numbers at any price. When the world stopped joining the church, then the believers multiplied. "And believers were the more added to the Lord, multitudes both of men and women" (Acts 5:14). This is a timeless lesson for evangelism also. The fewer unbelievers whom we pull into the church by coaxing and coercion, the greater the number of real believers will be. When we keep our motives pure and our appeals clean, God adds to the Church. There is always a multiplying of believers when there is less fleshly energy used to crowd the unconverted into the churches.

3. *A real revival will stamp out worldliness in the churches* (Acts 5:1-5). The church at Jerusalem was so dominated by the Holy Spirit, mastered by His love, and energized by His power, that it was impossible for impurities to live within it. When a man came into that assembly with a lie upon his lips and pretense in his heart, he could not live. Ananias was arrested and dropped dead. He could not live in that atmosphere with pretense in his soul. It is always a serious indictment against any church in which a person with a lie on his lips and pretense in his heart can live comfortably. Revival will bring a consciousness of the presence of the Holy Spirit. The Holy Spirit has a purifying effect upon the people. We do not hear enough today possibly about the cleansing, purifying effect of the fires of the Holy Spirit.

4. *We need revival today to reach the lost.* Nothing is as revitalizing to a Christian as to see a soul saved. Many Christians today are strangulated by immorality. They are curbed by ignorance. They have no knowledge of the living God. Greed for money on the part of individuals and na-

tions has brought distress. Only the purifying fires of revival can rid us of greed and immoral contamination and curb the waves of crime which threaten to inundate us.

When the breath of God comes upon us, miracles will take place and transformations will be witnessed which logic, arguments, and cold facts could not accomplish.

CHAPTER 2

THE REVIVAL AT SINAI
Exodus 32:1-35; 33:1-23

THE BACKGROUND OF REVIVAL

1. *The Hebrews were in slavery down in Egypt when Moses was born.* His father and mother were slaves, living under many circumscriptions and enduring great hardships. Many years before, God had promised that He would be with His people and deliver them from their bondage. God's method is often a man. If God chooses to use a man, He prepares him for the challenge. It was within the providence of God that Moses should receive the best possible training. God ordained that Moses would be reared by the royal family and receive the finest educational and cultural background available. His mother by no accident became his nurse and was paid for the work. Her guiding hand planted a deep concern in the soul of Moses. At the very first opportunity the gifted and conscientious young man identified himself with his people, the Hebrews (Exod. 2:11-20). God gave Moses further training in the wilderness for his colossal task. God's call to Moses to deliver the Hebrews from their bondage was as striking as his birth and childhood. Moses felt incompetent for the great challenge which God placed on his heart. This was not a bad sign. Moses raised many objections. God answered Moses' objections (Exod. 4:1-13) and gave him brilliant victories over Pharaoh (Exod., chaps. 7-14). Moses led the enslaved people to freedom. However, they needed more instructions and seasoning. While Moses and Joshua, his minister, and

their attendants went up into Mount Sinai to receive the law, the people lapsed momentarily into idolatry.

2. *The sin of the people* (Exod. 32:1-6).

(1) The occasion for the lapse into idolatry comes out of two things: the absence of Moses from the camp, and the idolatrous background of the people. Moses was up in Mount Sinai for forty days and forty nights (Exod. 24:18). He had not informed them of the length of his absence. This was a challenge to their faith and a test of their character. Some among them had doubtlessly longed for the worship of the false gods of Egypt. They had not dared to mention it while Moses was in the camp. His presence had served as a check on their licentious leanings. When Moses did not return after a reasonable length of time, it made way for the display of character. Their sincerity was placed on trial. It revealed the true disposition of the majority of the people. The absence of Moses provided a test of their allegiance.

(2) They requested Aaron to make gods to go before them (Exod. 32:1). The request was on the order of a command. They showed irreverence for Moses when they said, "As for this Moses" (vs. 1). This light and flippant language revealed ingratitude and rebellion. They declared that the cause of the request grew out of Moses' delayed return, but it went deeper than that. It was rooted in ignorance of God's purpose for them. Ignorance was back of the unrest. They based their actions on what they did not know.[1] "We wot not what is become of him" (vs. 1). They were not far enough removed from idolatry to forget it. All of these things combined moved them to appear before Aaron with a command.

(3) Aaron complied with the request (vs. 2). There is no implication here that Aaron tried to dissuade them. He executed their request with cordiality. He did not think he was forsaking God. When he had prepared the image of the calf, he declared a feast unto Jehovah (vs. 5). Aaron had worked out a syncretism. He made an effort to com-

bine Jehovah worship with the worship of Mnevis, the golden calf. of Egypt. Aaron and the people had much to learn. They had to learn that Jehovah requires absolute loyalty. He is a jealous God and will not share His glory with another.

(4) The people gladly took off their jewelry and earrings and gave them to Aaron to mold into an image. People intoxicated with vice spend freely to satisfy fleshly lusts. As this was true with the ancient people in the wilderness, it is true of our generation. They arose early in the morning to offer burnt offerings and to sit down to eat and drink. When they had finished eating and drinking, they arose to play. They were gratifying their own passions under the pretense of worship. This type of worship pleased them because it was fleshly and not spiritual. The great masses always prefer a type of worship which gives them fleshly gratification and sensual liberties. Many in the camp that day possibly looked on with horror and grief. They could not make themselves heard. The shout of the masses drowned their voices if they even dared to protest. The lapse at Sinai was an illustration of flesh asserting supremacy over faith, and of what happens to a people when that tragedy occurs.

3. *Disciplinary judgment* (vss. 15-28). Moses and Joshua entered the camp after God had informed Moses that while he was in the mountain the people had corrupted themselves. Moses interceded to God for them. When they came within hearing of the camp, Joshua thought he heard the cries of war. Evidently Moses had borne the burden alone with God. He had not talked to Joshua concerning his revelation from God. He had kept it down deep in his soul and had prayed earnestly. When God's people are gravely concerned and deeply moved, they often prefer to speak to God rather than men.

Moses threw the golden calf into the fire and melted it (vs. 20). The idol, the object of their adoration, had to be destroyed. The gold was melted, beaten to pieces, and strewn upon the waters. God shamed the people by making

clear the nothingness of their god. They were forced to de-
vour their own god. This was a severe punishment for them.
To consume the molten animals revered as deity among the
Egyptians was considered a thing of horror. The drinking
of the water where the powdered gold had been thrown
was not a revengeful act of Moses. It was not the hasty act
of anger. It was the punishment of God upon the people
for their idolatry. The people had an Egyptian background
and understood well the implications of this particular pro-
nouncement. It was a sickening thing to them. It was the
one way to teach them the folly of their acts.

Moses was very firm, and within hours after his arrival,
order prevailed within the camp. They saw in his face
horror, dismay, and grief mingled together. This mixed expression of Moses sobered the people. The idolaters stood
as if they had been rooted to the ground. They were fearful.

Moses rebuked Aaron (vs. 21). Moses asked Aaron,
"What did this people unto thee, that thou hast brought so
great a sin upon them?" (vs. 21). Moses considered Aaron
the chief author of the sin.[2] The weakness of Aaron's character is seen in the excuse he offered. Aaron placed the
blame for the sin on the people. This excuse is as old as the
Garden of Eden. It is a sign of weakness. It is the sign of
one who has fallen to temptation and then is childish enough
to blame others. It shows the lack of manliness to make an
honest confession of guilt. Aaron was responsible for the
people. This is a serious indictment against religious leaders who let their followers grow worldly. Religious leaders
are accountable before God for the sins of their people.
When leaders are without courage, the people perish. Aaron
had faced a senseless mob. They had stood before him with
hard faces. He might have been stoned if he had not complied with their wishes. However, it would have been better
to die than to destroy the people. They did not stone Moses
when he stood firm. Often religious leaders excuse themselves by saying, "The society of our day is entirely evil.
The people will not listen. It does no good to try to correct

them. We must indulge them." This was the sin of Aaron and it will destroy a people.

The disciplinary judgment of God (vss. 27-28). Three thousand were slain with the sword. This was not the will of Moses. It was the will of God for Moses declared, "Thus saith the LORD God of Israel . . . ." This was a harsh thing, but idolatry is harsh. It often requires harsh methods to awaken people. They had a law against idolatry (Exod. 20:23). The people had pledged to obey the law (Exod. 24:3). They had heard it forbidden among the thunders of Sinai (Exod. 20:4-5). If all the people who participated in the worship of Mnevis, the golden calf, had died, it still would have been justice. It was the mercy of God that spared any of them.

THE REVIVAL

1. *The awakening factor.*[3] The awakening factor was God's threat of withdrawal. God said, "I will not go up in the midst of thee" (Exod. 33:3). The people had sinned a grievous sin at Sinai, and Moses had prayed earnestly unto God. After his second intercession, Moses had received a concession from God (32:34). God had promised not to destroy the people for their sin, and would permit Moses to lead them into the Land of Promise. The Lord had added, however, that He would not go up in the midst of them. This shocked them. This awakened them to the realization of the problems which they faced.

2. *They needed three things.*

(1) They needed conviction. Until people are convicted that they are wrong and that they are out of relation with the true God, they are not likely to respond in a wholesome fashion. God began by calling them a "stiffnecked people" (33:5). God did not speak to them in a general way. He designated their sin as well as their inner attitude. It is often necessary to be direct. The prophet Nathan brought conviction to David when he said unto him, "Thou art the man" (II Sam. 12:7). The prophet let David think the matter over, then pass his own judgment and phrase his

judgment in words of condemnation. After that he pointed
the finger directly at him and told him that he was the very
man upon whom he had already passed judgment. God's
message to the sinners in this revival was pointed and direct. God's message to sinners in every hour is pointed and
direct. The message must be so delivered that the individual
listening will feel that the evangelist is familiar with his
own case and is speaking personally to him.

(2) They needed to be shocked (Exod. 33:3).
When God threatened to travel with them no more and to
hide His face from them, they were shocked. They had
seen God deliver them with a high hand by sending judgment on the Egyptians. They had seen the waters of the
Jordan stand back. They had seen God feed them with
manna. If God was to travel no more with them, they
would be doomed. It shocked them. Their perverseness led
God to see that they were unfit for His near presence. God
hid His face from them. When the Lord hides His face
from the people, it could signify two or three different
things.

(a) It might signify the judgment of God.[4] It
was a judgment when God drove Adam and Eve from the
Garden (Gen. 3:24). It took on the form of a judgment when
God answered Saul no more and Saul went to the witch of
Endor for instruction (I Sam. 28:6). It is a judgment upon
any people when God withdraws as behind a cloud and no
longer lets His light shine on the preaching, organization,
and activities of the churches.

(b) The withdrawn presence of God may be an
act of mercy.[5] In this case, it is inferred that it was an act
of mercy because God said, "Lest I consume thee in the
way" (Exod. 33:3). The sun hardens clay, but it melts
butter. The near-burning presence of God will purify one
and deaden another. The presence of God softened and
made lovable the life of John, whereas it hardened and made
a traitor of Judas. In the white-hot heat of revival, when
God is very near, we all have seen this very thing. We have
seen some, in the season of soul refreshing, melt and come

to God to find salvation; while we have seen others harden themselves, fight against God, and drift out to go to hell.

There always comes a time when man at his best is not equal to the problems which he faces. When that time comes, it is God or disaster. Such a time had come to the people of Sinai.

In answer to the urgent request of Moses, God had promised to send His angel before them (vs 2). The angel which was to travel before them may have been a symbol of the presence of the Holy Spirit, but it was not the presence of the Holy Spirit because the Holy Spirit is God. They needed divine protection and divine guidance. They would still have divine guidance in the form of the directing angel, but it would not be the absolute presence of God. It would only be an endorsement of what they were doing and a symbol of God's presence.

(3) The people needed instruction[6] (vs. 5). The instruction of God was plain. He declared that they were stubborn and that their stubborn attitude threatened to engulf them. It is never kind to hide the real condition of people from themselves. It is cruel to give people bouquets of flowers when they should have bolts of judgment. Soft and conciliatory messages never bring conviction and repentance to the people. The Lord also instructed them to put off their ornaments. This was not only a call for sacrifice, but this was a definite blast at their pride.

3. *The Word of God was declared* (vss. 1-5). Moses told the people what God said. "For the LORD had said unto Moses, Say unto the children of Israel" (vs. 5). Moses did not claim to be the author of these commands and directions. He was the spokesman for God. He stood with God and spoke the mind and will of God. At no place does Moses claim to be the author of the directives given in verses 1 and 5 of chapter 33. It was necessary that the people know the mind of God and the will of God. Through the Word of God they learned these vital things. In this very first revival, of which we have enough material to study, we find the Word of God playing a prominent role.

4. *Renewed interest in worship* (vss. 7-11). "Moses took the tabernacle, and pitched it without the camp, afar off. . . . And it came to pass, that every one which sought the LORD went out unto the tabernacle of the congregation, which was without the camp" (vs. 7). The focus of power for the revival was the "tent of meeting." The focus of power for the revival under Elijah was the top of Mount Carmel. The focus of power at Pentecost was in the open street. The focus of power for the great revival under White-field and Wesley, known as the Evangelical Revival in England, and the Great Awakening in America, was the open-air service. They preached to the great crowds in the fields. In this generation, Billy Graham has become a "stadium" preacher. No place except the large football stadiums will accommodate the crowds who are hungry to hear the timely message of Billy Graham.

God had not revoked His decision to withdraw. Moses hoped to keep wrestling with God on the matter, trusting that God would revoke it. He could not keep going to Sinai, so he erected the "tent of meeting."

(1) The tent was located outside the camp afar off (vs. 7). We do not know why the tent of meeting was placed outside the camp, unless it was due to the fact that the camp had been polluted and the Lord had threatened to withdraw His presence. Therefore, He would not come into the midst of the people. Moses placed the tent outside the camp. He spent part of the time in the tent and part of the time in the camp in contact with the people. It was a method of securing renewed life for the people. The tent was called the "tent of meeting," and the people were urged to go out of the camp to the tent and meet God in prayer.[7] Location in this case was very important. Generally location of places of worship is significant, but what a people do and what they offer has more to do with attracting the crowds and meeting their needs than the location of the place of worship. Any restaurant that prepares its food well and serves it efficiently and courteously will always have many customers, regardless of its location. The same thing is true

with a place of worship. The people are more interested in what they receive and the way they receive it than they are in location. Cambuslang, on the outskirts of Glasgow, in 1742, was a small town of about nine hundred people. A great awakening took place in that small town. The pastor was William McCulloch. He was not a popular preacher. His delivery was slow, but his message was biblical. At the request of the people, the pastor began to hold a few special meetings each week in which the Word of God was expounded. Finally, the interest became so intense that they threw open the doors of the church, and every day for twelve weeks he preached daily to a stricken people. The news of the revival spread until it became the talk of Scotland. People came in great numbers from all parts of the land to see the grace of God. Often the attendance was as large as ten thousand, and a few times it surpassed thirty thousand. This took place in a little town of approximately nine hundred people. It is a striking demonstration of the power of God, and it also enheartens those who may think that their churches are poorly located. Wherever God is and wherever the grace of God is manifest, people will gather and great good will be done.

(2) The meaning of the tent of worship to the people (vs 7). It became a place of contact with God. "Every one which sought the LORD went out into the tabernacle of the congregation, which was without the camp." Moses had urged individuals and families to seek the Lord. There had been no special place nor time for prayer, and they had neglected to pray. They had left the praying to Moses. Here we find them turning to personal religion. It is revealing that in this very first recorded revival in history we have an emphasis on personal religion. The people were not going to God through Moses, Joshua, Aaron, or anyone else, but they were going directly to God. The people no doubt worshiped God in their own tents and they may have worshiped in other places, but in this particular case everyone who sought the Lord went into the tent of meeting. Anyone at any time may be able to find the Lord out in the

woods or in his own home, but worship is always more conducive in a tent of meeting where the Gospel is presented in song and sermon.

The tent was a place of contact with God, but it was also a place of prayer and surrender. Jacob had stayed away from God's house for twenty years, but when the Lord commanded him, he went back and built an altar unto the Lord. He and his entire family fell down before the altar and worshiped God in prayer and thanksgiving. Jacob and his family might have surrendered to the will of God and might have prayed to God almost anywhere, but the altar seems to have been more conducive to prayer and worship. In every revival there has been a focus of power.

(3) The tent of meeting had a very definite meaning for Moses. It was a place of revelation for him. The tent was outside the camp and might have been a reminder that God was no longer among the people.[8] The ark was a symbol of the nearness of God. The people were urged to enter the tent and pray unto God. Moses and the people came to the tent to plead for the near presence of Jehovah. The tent was called "the tent of the testimony" (Num. 9:15). It is possible that the tent housed the ark, but the tent was an instrument in its own right. The account says that the "LORD talked with Moses" (Exod. 33:9). In the tent of meeting, Moses had close communion with Jehovah. Moses, as any other man, was at his best when he touched God.

The tent of meeting meant also a regular habit for Moses. "Moses went out unto the tabernacle" (Exod. 33:8). The fact that it was a regular habit of Moses made an indelible impression upon his people. The people saw him go in and out before them. They saw him as he spent part of his time in the tent and part of the time in his own home or office of operation.

When Moses went to the tent of worship, it became a time of reverence. When Moses entered the tent, "all the people rose up" (Exod. 33:8). This shows the power of example. The people observed their religious leaders. When Moses entered the tent, "the cloudy pillar descended, and

stood at the door of the tabernacle" (vs. 9). This was a
sign of God's approval. It also signified the presence of God.

Tent worship prepared Moses for the task ahead. When
he had finished speaking face to face with God as one friend
speaks to another, "he turned again into the camp" (vs. 11).
Moses went back into the camp to perform his office work.
Worship was central in this revival. Both the leaders and
the people worshiped God at an appointed place. As they
prayed unto God, as they worshiped God, and as they
waited in the presence of God, their hearts were prepared
for God to do a work of grace.

5. *Repentance was primal in this revival.*[9] The twofold evidence of true repentance is set forth in verse 4.
"When the people heard these evil tidings, they mourned."
Repentance is more than a morbid sorrow, but it is a sorrow. When people mourn for their sins, that is part of
repentance. These people mourned for the sin which had
provoked God to withdraw from them. They felt that the
threat of God's withdrawal from them was far greater punishment than the disciplinary judgment which He had sent
upon them in the death of more than three thousand of
their compatriots. We do not find that they mourned over
the death of the three thousand, but when God denied them
His favorable presence, then they mourned.[10] The bitterest
consequence of sin is God's departure from the sinner. God
had promised them that they could have the land that
flowed with milk and honey, but they could feel no joy
over such an accession as long as God's presence would be
denied.

The second evidence of their repentance is seen in their
outward response. "And the children of Israel stripped
themselves of their ornaments by the mount Horeb" (vs 6).
The removal of the ornaments was a mark of mourning, and
these ornaments were possibly removed and given to deco-
rate the tent.[11] Actions are always more meaningful than
words. The people not only mourned in their hearts that
God had withdrawn from them, but they were willing to act
upon the impulses which flooded their souls. Great crowds

came out during the ministry of John the Baptist. They. came from Jerusalem and all Judea and the regions round about Jordan. As they heard him, they were convicted, confessed their sins, and were baptized. Along with them, came many of the leading Pharisees and Sadducees who asked for baptism, but John said unto them, "Bring forth therefore fruits meet for repentance" (Matt. 3:8). John said in effect, "Your presence and the fact that you have presented yourself at the altar is not enough. You must show actions worthy of your words." What John the Baptist centuries later preached to the people in Judea was thoroughly in keeping with the type of repentance manifest here. It was an inner transformation followed by outward actions. Jacob at Shechem had buried the symbols of the false gods under the oak tree. It is necessary that sins be put aside, that they be buried under the blood of Christ, that they be forsaken by the sinner. It is not surprising to find that repentance is primal in the very first revival in history of which we have enough information to discuss. Repentance is a turning to God from evil. It is a turning to God from sin. It is not a turning from sin to God. For turning from sin to God indicates that one has the ability to break with sin and then turn to God. This is not true. One must turn to God as God works the grace of repentance in him. As he turns to God, then God breaks the claims and shackles of sin and sets him free.

6. *Prayer is prominent in the revival.* Besides the prayer of the people in their tents and the tent of meeting, there are recorded here at least three intercessory prayers by Moses.

(1) The first intercessory prayer by Moses is found in Exodus 32:11-14. As soon as Moses received the instruction from God of the corruption of his people, he began to plead with God concerning His wrath against the people. He pleaded with God not to be wrathful against the people whom He had brought up out of Egypt with great power, indicating that with the same power which He had brought them up, He could also sustain them, even in spite

of their sins. He also very tactfully reminded Jehovah of the scorn of the Egyptians, how the Egyptians would speak against God, saying that He had led the people out into the mountains to slay them. He urged upon God to remember the promise which He had made to Abraham, Isaac, and Israel, His servants, to multiply their seed as the stars of heaven and to give them a land to inherit. This warm, searching, and direct pleading of Moses got results. The Lord decided not to destroy the people, but merely to send a harsh and disciplinary judgment upon them.

(2) The second intercessory prayer (32:31-32). After God had executed a sore punishment upon the people for their lapse into idolatry, then Moses went before God with his second intercessory prayer. He confessed the sins of his people. He said, "Oh, this people have sinned a great sin" (vs. 31). Then he pleaded with God for forgiveness of the people. "Yet now, if thou wilt forgive their sin —; and if not, blot me, I pray thee, out of thy book which thou hast written" (vs. 32). God's reply to the pleading leader was that He would punish the people for their sins, but that He would permit Moses to lead the people of Israel into the land which He had promised them. The angel would go before him, but God Himself would not go. The Lord further said that He would plague the people because of the calf of gold.

(3) The third intercessory prayer (33:12-16). The pleadings of Moses in this intercessory prayer, as well as in the others, is a great example of tender, earnest logic and concern. One never read or heard a prayer more personal or direct to the heart of God. The essence of the prayer is very simple and pointed. Moses said in essence: You asked me to bring the people from Egypt. The project is of You. I did not originate the idea. You said that I had found grace in Thy sight. Now if I have found grace in Thy sight, show me Thy way. Show me Thy plan; do not leave me in uncertainty as to Thy intentions concerning this people or as to the angel whom Thou will give to guide. If I have found grace in Thy sight, let it become a reality.[12] Moses' faith is

not shaken, but he seeks knowledge. He seeks more revelation. He is saying to Jehovah, "I do not understand. Show
me Thy way." Moses pleads with God, "Your presence sets
my people apart from all the peoples of the earth. It is the
distinguishing mark." God had promised to send an angel
before them, but this was not enough to satisfy Moses. He
wanted God's presence for his people. Moses identified himself with his people. This is the mind of a true and effective
religious leader. Moses asked nothing for himself, but all for
his people. This intercession not only reveals the place of
prayer in this great revival, but it reveals the kind of praying that brings revival. In the midst of God's wrath, Moses
could have turned his back upon his people because God
promised Moses that He would turn His face away from the
people of Israel and make of Moses a great nation, for God
said, "And I will make of thee a great nation" (32:10). True
religious leaders and revivalists seek no honor, no position,
no name, and no praise for themselves. They seek salvation
for their people.

This warm, searching, direct intercessory prayer of
Moses got results. God replied to him, "My presence shall go
with thee, and I will give thee rest" (33:14). In the Hebrew
language, the word for presence of God is the word "face."
The heart of the great religious leader was thrilled with the
words of God, giving assurance that His face would be with
them. But Moses dared to go a little further and said, "If thy
presence [face] go not with me, carry us not up hence" (vs.
15). Moses does not mean to express doubt in God's assurance, but he expresses a feeling of insufficiency. Moses did
not know what minute the people might burst again into
rebellion and idolatry. He further prayed, therefore, that his
people be distinguished from all other peoples on the earth,
that God be patient with them, and that God go with them.
Moses was saying in effect that he had rather die where he
stood than to go anywhere without the presence of God. In
verse 17 God assured Moses that this request would be
granted.

Moses then waxed very bold and said, "Shew me thy

glory" (vs. 18). Moses wanted a revelation surpassing any preceding revelation.[13] He wanted a revelation which would go even beyond Jehovah talking face to face with him. When he spoke face to face with God, he saw a "similitude of Jehovah" (Num. 12:8), the manifestation of the glory of God in a certain form and not the essential glory of God. He saw the glory of God reflected on the clouds or as it shone through the cloud. Moses desired to behold the Being of God. God let him behold His goodness, but not His face. Moses had seen much of the glory of God when he spoke face to face with Him in the fiery cloud at Sinai and when God in the bush aflame in the desert had spoken to him. He had seen the great glory of God as God overthrew Pharaoh's army in the sea. He had witnessed the great glory of God again and again, but the appetite always grows on what it feeds. If one feeds on the wisdom, presence, and glory of God, his appetite will ever increase for more and more glory, and more and more of the wisdom, presence, and power of God. If one is a little soul and feeds upon the frivolous things around him, more and more he will become a part of what he feasts upon.

The Lord answered Moses' request in part. God told Moses that there was a place by Himself upon the rock. He told Moses that He would place him in the cleft of the rock and would cover him with His hand while He passed by. He would give Moses a chance to see something of His glory, but Moses would not see His face. He would only see the afterglow. The face of God is reserved to be shown to the redeemed as one of the great rewards which awaits them in the land beyond the sky.

God wills to be importuned for what it does for the earnest seeker. Moses and his people searched their own hearts and poured themselves out like water on the ground. In the long days of prayer, a change took place in their attitude and souls that God could honor by revoking the threat. The prayers of Moses and the prayers of the people were fervent. They were not mere cold repetitions; not prayers uttered by Buddha machines, or symbolized by burning candles, or expressions of worn and meaningless platitudes. They were the effectual, fervent desires of burning hearts. This sort of prayer characterized the revival at Sinai.

As a result of this revival, the people were given spiritual impetus to move on from the wilderness toward the Land of Promise. It gave them fortitude and strength to stand up against the vicissitudes they were certain to further face in the wilderness. Here in this very first of all the great revivals, we find three or four things standing out. The Word of God was prominent. A great doctrine, the doctrine of repentance, was primal. The place of worship in evangelism was established. The necessity of prayer was demonstrated.

CHAPTER 3

THE REVIVAL UNDER SAMUEL

I Samuel 7:1-17

The revival under Samuel began in the heart of a consecrated woman at least a generation before it actually took
place. Revival may break out any time, but it always starts
in a praying heart. In bitterness of soul, Hannah prayed
sincerely to God (I Sam. 1:10). Hannah was one of the two
wives of Elkanah. She was childless. Barrenness was a grief
to all the Hebrew women. Hannah was driven to the altar
out of grief and embarrassment. She asked God for a son.
This was not a new nor a remarkable practice for a Hebrew
woman, but the remarkable thing is that she dedicated the
unborn son to the Lord even before his conception (vs. 11).
She prayed so earnestly that Eli, the priest, thought she was
drunk. It was not uncommon for drunken women to wander
into the place of worship. It was a time of low morals for
both sexes. When Eli discovered that she was truly praying,
he pledged to join her in prayer for a son.

God answered this prayer and as soon as the child Samuel
was old enough, Hannah brought him to the house of the
Lord in Shiloh and left him with Eli. Hannah's reward was
in the popular temple life of her son. It is better to instill
one's highest ideals in his child than to write a best seller.
Samuel received his earliest impressions of God from his
praying mother. It would be interesting to read history to
see the place of women in all great movements. Mothers,
wives, and sisters have influenced their men directly or indi-
rectly in almost all great history-making movements.

45

CHARACTERISTICS OF THE AGE

1. *Religious corruption led to spiritual destitution* (I Sam. 2:12-17). The priest sons of Eli perverted the law. They changed the system of sacrifice to suit themselves. Instead of using a three-pronged fork to dip up the sodden flesh for themselves, they sent servants to demand of the worshipers unsodden and raw flesh (vs. 15). This was contrary to temple customs. When the conscientious sacrificers demurred, Eli's priest sons would take the flesh by force (I Sam. 2:14). This practice caused the Hebrews to abhor the offering of the Lord (vs. 17). It provoked God to revoke His promise to Eli and his family (vs. 30). Spiritual confusion and dissatisfaction characterized the period before the invasion of the Philistines.

2. *It was a period of intellectual blindness* (I Sam. 3:1, 4:1-11). "The word of the LORD was precious in those days; there was no open vision" (3:1). God refused to speak to the people through the unclean lips of Hophni and Phinehas. When the people have no access to the Word of God, they become intellectually blind. They lose their vision. In the days of Amos, the people were without the Word of God because they refused to hear it; but in the days of Eli's sons, they were without it because God refused to give it. In both instances, the results were intellectual darkness.

When internal confusion exists, it disqualifies the people for conflict from without. The Philistines invaded Israel. The Hebrews went against them in battle at Ebenezer, and Israel was smitten. Some four thousand of their men were slain (I Sam. 4:2). The elders suggested that the ark of the covenant be removed from Shiloh and carried into battle. They thought it might save them from defeat since it was a token of the presence of God (4:3). This was a sure sign of intellectual blindness. To take the ark into battle was an act of idolatry. By such actions, they showed that they looked on the ark as a fetish or as a charm of good luck. The Hebrews mistook a token of the presence of God for the actual presence of God. This in itself revealed blindness. The misuse of the ark did not help them. It was the undoing of them. They were defeated by the enemies more thoroughly than before. In this battle they lost thirty thousand men (4:10). The ark was captured (vs. 11). This was a rash thing which they had done. The ark was a symbol of the presence of God and was used in observing the Day of Atonement. This act separated the ark from the rest of the sacred furniture in the temple at Shiloh. Rashness and foolhearted decisions are the fruits of intellectual nearsightedness.

The ark became a curse to the Philistines. When it was placed in the temple at Ashdod beside Dagon, the false god, a strange thing happened. The next morning, the temple attendants found the image of Dagon fallen upon his face before the ark of the Lord. They set him upright; but the following morning he was again found lying flat before the ark of the Lord, this time with his head and both hands broken off. This threw a great fear into the people of Ashdod. They were smitten with boils and became very ill. These two effects of the presence of the ark made a tremendous impression upon these Philistines. The false god Dagon had fallen before the ark of the Lord, and infections in the form of boils had not only made the people ill, but had killed many of them. The ark was taken to Gath, where great destruction came upon the people and many died with emerods (I Sam. 5:9-10). When they removed the ark of the Lord to Ekron, the same plague struck as the ark entered the city. The Philistines complained so bitterly at the presence of the ark that the lords of the Philistines were compelled to take definite action. The priests and diviners of the Philistines advised that if the ark should be returned, an offering must accompany it (6:3). The offering was to consist of "five golden emerods and five golden mice" (6:4). It appears from this that they had been plagued with a devastating invasion of field mice, as well as boils (6:4-5). The extraordinary voracity of field mice, as well as the unbelievable rate at which they multiply, has been noted by many writers of natural history. Aristotle in his *History of Animals*, volume I, page 37, tells how mice often multiplied with such rapidity that they would destroy an entire crop within a few hours. One day a crop of corn would be ripe and ready to garner, and the very next day it would be completely destroyed by field mice.[1] The offering of golden mice and boils by the Philistines had nothing to do with talismans made by the magicians to effect curses or avert evils.

The Philistines decided upon an ingenious device. They would place the ark, with the jewels for a trespass offering, on a cart. They would take two milk cows, which had never worn a yoke, and tie the cows to the cart, placing their young calves in a pen nearby. Then they would turn the cows loose. If the cows, unaccustomed to the yoke, drew the cart and if, in spite of their natural instinct, they deserted their calves and took the cart directly to Beth-shemesh, then the Philistines could conclude that Jehovah had sent the evil upon them. But if the cows wandered aimlessly around, then they would know that it was not the hand of the God of the Hebrews upon them. Without human guidance, the cows went straight to Beth-shemesh (6:12). So the Philistines concluded that the cows were directed in a supernatural way. Beth-shemesh meant literally "house of the sun." It was a priestly city, called Beth-dagon (Josh. 15:41), on the border of the tribe of Judah (Josh. 15:10) about twelve miles from Ekron.

Judgment fell upon the people at Beth-shemesh. "He smote the men of Beth-shemesh, because they had looked into the ark of the Lord (I Sam. 6:19). They gazed upon the ark with profane curiosity.[2] They should have covered the ark with proper material, but instead they left it exposed to public gaze. This brought down the judgment of God to vindicate His holiness. (Even the priests and Levites were not to gaze upon the furniture of the Holy of Holies.) A large number died. Dr. A. F. Kirkpatrick in the *Cambridge Bible* says that there may be a discrepancy in the number reported smitten.[3] Since the population of the city of Beth-shemesh is not likely to have been as many as fifty thousand, it is possible that such a mistake could have crept into the text, but we have no way of knowing the exact population of the area nor how long the ark was exposed to public gaze. Since we do not know how long the celebration lasted nor the thousands who might have come from near and far to join in the celebration of the return of the ark, we are inclined to go along with the ancient text.

The ark was removed to Kirjath-jearim, i.e., "city of forest." It was a city in a densely wooded area. The name was equivalent to Woodville.[4] Kirjath-jearim originally belonged to the Gibeonites (Josh. 15:9). It was located about nine miles from Beth-shemesh. It was in the hills and on much higher ground than Beth-shemesh.

3. *Heart hunger for Jehovah.* "Israel lamented after the LORD" (I Sam. 7:2). The revival began about twenty years after the ark was removed to Kirjath-jearim. The twenty years referred to in verse 2 do not signify the length of time the ark stayed at Kirjath-jearim, but the length of time before the people reached a state of real repentance.[5] These twenty years marked a dreary period in Israel's history. Politically, the Israelites were vassals of the Philistines. Religiously, they were unrelated and confused. The tabernacle was dismantled, and the ark was in a private home (vs. 1). Samuel did nothing during these twenty years about removing the ark to some central place of worship. He left it in Abinadab's private house in Kirjath-jearim. Shiloh was probably in the hands of the Philistines or it may have been completely destroyed. Since the nation was a vassal to the Philistines, Samuel was limited in many respects. He might have taken the position that it was not the time to set up a central place of worship for he was not able to make the people sensitive to their wickedness. He felt that this was a prerequisite to a restoration of free access to God. It is likely that the daily offerings and other sacred services were being offered at Nob during this period. (I Sam. 21). During the last part of the twenty-year period, Samuel was growing in influence as he moved among the people and preached with telling effect. His prophet's labors bore fruit. "Israel lamented after the LORD" (vs. 2) is a revealing statement. The people were repentant. They were not repentant because they were vassals to Philistia nor because they were religiously disjointed, but because of the preaching of Samuel.

METHODS OF THE REVIVAL

1. *Itinerant preaching* (vs. 3). "And Samuel spake unto all the house of Israel." Samuel went from place to place. He spoke in the towns, villages and countrysides, for no large public gathering had as yet been called. Wherever Samuel went, he seems to have brought the same message. Since the method of communication was limited in those days, it was necessary for him to take the time and energy to travel from place to place wherever the people were and to take the message directly to them. The sum and substance of his message is found in verse 3, and it is very likely that he emphasized one or all of these points in almost every sermon which he gave to the people in the towns and villages.

2. *A direct message* (7:3).

(1) He called upon the people to "put away the strange gods and Ashtaroth." This was a direct attack upon idolatry. "The strange gods" referred to Baal (vs. 4). The plural indicates the multiplicity of these idols. These gods were worshiped under the name of Baal-Zebub, Baal-Peor, Baal-Berith, etc. Baal was the sun-god of Phoenicia. Ashtaroth was the female goddess of the grove. The origin of this goddess was Babylon. The image was a wooden column or an image of the sacred tree of Assyria. Though Ashtaroth was the goddess of battle and triumphs, the worship was sensual and generally gave rise to immorality.

The Israelites were drawn to the worship of strange gods by its fleshly and fascinating effects upon them. The worship of Jehovah was simple, reverent, severe, and self-denying. The worship of the false gods was lively and attractive. They indulged fashionable entertainment and fleshly revelries. It appealed to the carnal mind. The contrast is quite similar to that found in many quarters today between Protestant and Roman worship. When Samuel urged them to put away Baal and Ashtaroth, he abjured that which was fashionable. It was a call to return to the solemn and somber worship of Jehovah. To many of the Jews it was a sign of narrowness. They were liberal in thought and practice. The entire religious atmosphere smacked of liberalism. To become exclusively devoted to Jehovah was narrow. This type of liberalism had proved to have a disintegrating effect on the Hebrew religion. Samuel, therefore, urged them to put away every image and every symbol connected with the worship of Baal. God would receive them in no other way.

"And Ashtaroth" (vs. 3). It is significant that he had singled out Ashtaroth. Ashtaroth was their most beloved goddess. It was their darling. True repentance always strikes at the darling sin. The battle for a soul is not fought around a flock of sins. The battle for a soul is fought around one sin. When the victory over that one particular sin is won, then the others will go. Each age has its darling sin. With the Hebrews it was Ashtaroth. With the Americans today it may be Sabbath desecration. Any evangelist who does not strike at the darling sin is not likely to bring conviction to the people.

(2) "Serve him only" (vs. 3). They must be out and out for God. They must be wholly for God and no other. They should serve only God, or they could not serve Him at all. They must empty their hands of false gods, and they must fill their hands with service to the Lord. They had been delivered into the hands of the Philistines because they had turned away from worshiping only God. They had indulged in the sensual worship of the false gods, and they must now denounce idolatry and return completely unto God, or they would not receive God's deliverance.

"Prepare your hearts unto the LORD" (vs. 3). It was a good sign that the people had begun to denounce evil practices and resolve within themselves to turn from them; but that in itself was not enough. The heart must be prepared against the sins which once ruled there. The individual must turn from anything that would weaken his resistance or pull him back into the grip of the former sins. He must fortify himself against the old temptations. He must fill the heart, which was so recently emptied of devotion to evil, with positive truth and good. He must thoroughly align himself with the cause of righteousness. If the heart is left empty, Satan will soon re-enter, and the last state will be worse than the first (Luke 11:26). Samuel was quite aware of this danger. No doubt he worked tirelessly to place this positive emphasis.

(3) He sounded a note of victory. "And he will deliver you out of the hand of the Philistines" (vs. 3). If the people would follow this positive instruction and come again to trust God and only God, He would deliver them from the hands of the Philistines. They had been worshiping at the altar of Baal, who was generally known as the god of might, and yet he had been impotent to help them. They had worshiped in the groves and bowed down before Ashtaroth, who was known as the goddess of battles and victories, and yet they were in worse condition than they had ever been since they left the bondage of Egypt. The prophet is calling upon them to turn away from a trust in the philosophies of men and he pleads that they positively depend upon the living God. If they would do this, they would receive the victory for which they so longed.

3. *Samuel called a general assembly at Mizpeh* (vs. 5). The word Mizpeh means "the watchtower." It belonged originally to the tribe of Benjamin (Josh. 18:26). The site is not definitely identified but it is either a hill 2,935 feet high, which lies five miles northwest of Jerusalem, or "Scopus," a broad ridge directly north of Jerusalem. There is convincing argument for either one of the locations. Since the mountain five miles to the northwest bears the name of Samuel, it appears to many that this undoubtedly is the correct place. However, the ridge north of Jerusalem, known as Scopus, is considered by the majority as the place because the word "Scopus" means "watchman." At any rate, Mizpeh, near Jerusalem, is not to be confused with the Mizpeh in Gilead (Judg. 10:17). On other important occasions, the people had been gathered at Mizpeh during this period. The declaration of war against Benjamin took place at Mizpeh (Judg. 20). The people gathered at Mizpeh when Saul was elected king (I Sam. 10:17), and also many years later when

Judas Maccabaeus led Israel to revolt against Antiochus Epiphanes.[6]

The people had put away the strange gods which were among them. They were repentant. Samuel knew the impact and power of an assembly of folk who were like-minded and whose experiences were similar. Spiritual convictions would be deepened and repentance made more intense by such an assembly. Samul knew the state of mind of the people. He had been among them continuously. He saw the possibilities of a great revival. He believed the best method at this stage was an assembly. His judgment was correct. When the people came together at Mizpeh, the stage was set with all the essentials for a mighty spiritual awakening. The revival was on — swift as lightning it came. Revival generally comes like a clap of thunder and with the speed of light. The conditions were met, and God responded with revival.

Mizpeh was inevitable. There might have been revival without the gathering, but the assembly at Mizpeh seems to have been one of the vital things which brought about the revival. When the atmospheric conditions in the heavens are right for precipitation, rain is inevitable. All the elements for a revival were in existence, and the laws of the Spirit moved toward Mizpeh. It is not really a question of whether there would have been a revival if there had been no assemblage at Mizpeh, but was it possible not to have a Mizpeh? Revival spirit was in ferment in the land, and the same God who gave rise to that spirit directed Samuel. It is sufficient to say Samuel promoted repentance and revival among his people, and the methods used were blessed of God. It appears that four things of significance took place at the assembly of Mizpeh.

(1) They were called to a dedication (vs. 6). "And drew water, and poured it out before the LORD." This particular act has no parallel in the Old Testament. The Targum paraphrases this experience by making it read, "poured out their hearts in repentance." It signified contrition for sin, but it went further than contrition and humility. It definitely was a dedication. Water poured out on the ground cannot

be gathered up again. Lives dedicated to God are dedicated for always. They are not to be taken back. When one dedicates himself to God, he is not to gather himself up again and use his energies for his own ends.

(2) They fasted at Mizpeh (vs. 6). Just as they fasted on the Day of Atonement (Lev. 16:29), so they fasted at Mizpeh in the spirit of contrition and humility. They were expressing repentance by doing without food and thus afflicting their bodies.

(3) They confessed their sins. They said, "We have sinned against the LORD" (vs. 6). Their confession was made publicly because they had sinned in public. They recognized that their sins primarily were against God, and they confessed that they had sinned against God. They took shame unto themselves and they gave glory unto God. God had done so many things for them in the past, and yet they had been so shortsighted. They had so soon forgotten the good things of God. Now they were sorry that they had turned away from God and that they had forgotten His tender mercies. When conviction gets so deep that people begin to confess their sins, a revival is in that place.

A small rural church in the South was recently endeavoring to have a revival. The preaching was fair, the singing was good, and the attendance was most excellent, but very few were being saved. Nothing of revival proportions was taking place, but conviction was becoming more and more intense throughout the entire community. During one of the morning services two men, seated on opposite sides of the building, who had not spoken to each other for seventeen years because of serious trouble years ago, got up simultaneously and started toward each other. They met each other in the center of the auditorium, and putting their arms around each other, shook hands, forgave each other, and made up. When these men became so convicted that they were willing to confess their sins and forgive each other publicly, revival broke out. Every lost person in the entire community, except one man, accepted Christ as Saviour and was baptized into the fellowship of the church at the close of the revival. It was one of the most far-reaching revivals ever witnessed in that rural area. The same thing that took place in that rural church took place at Mizpeh. The people not only confessed that they had wronged God, but it is very likely that they confessed their sins and their selfishness to each other.

It is never wise to use a set system in revival services. It is fine to have a system of worship and to have a form of worship, but we should always be open to the leadership of the Spirit of God to lay aside any program or any system which we may be following, if God indicates. The writer saw revival break out several years ago in a church in a south Texas city because the pastor of the church was willing to be led of the Spirit of God. Right in the middle of that revival effort he permitted people to stand up and give their testimony. During the testimony period, one lady stood up and literally confessed her selfishness and her sins. She was a member of the church, but she had not had the right spirit nor had she lived as God would have a Christian to live. She had the conviction and courage to confess it. It was in that minute that revival began in that church. Others began to confess, and God's people got right with themselves and with the Lord. As a result, there was a great outpouring of the Spirit of God, and many people were saved and united with the church during that effort. As many as fifty people joined the church in one service. The majority of those were on profession of faith. It was the opinion of the pastor that the revival actually started in these moments of confession when God's people publicly confessed their wrongs. One does not have to confess to his brethren nor does he have to stand up in public and tell how mean he feels himself to be, unless God definitely directs him. But in all cases he must actually confess his sins to the Lord. "If we confess our sins, he is faithful and just to forgive us our sins, and to cleanse us from all unrighteousness" (I John 1:9). This statement was made directly to Christians.

(4) Samuel judged the people at Mizpeh. "And Samuel judged" (vs. 6). The assembly lasted many days. We do not know how long. It was long enough for the

Philistines to gather an army for battle, and it was long enough for God's people to get right with the Lord. It was long enough for revival to ferment. During this time Samuel judged the people. We have no knowledge as to what constituted the actions of Samuel as he judged the people, but we may be sure that it had a definite part in developing the proper spirit for revival at the assembly.

4. *Prayer prevailed at Mizpeh* (I Sam. 7:8). When the Philistines heard that the children of Israel had gathered at Mizpeh, the lords of the Philistines led their forces against Israel. The Philistines regarded such an assembly by one of their vassals as a step toward a revolt. They marshalled an army and marched on Mizpeh. The Philistines were correct in a way. A revival was in progress at Mizpeh, and revival always gives birth to the urge for freedom. The Philistines, being suspicious of the gathering at Mizpeh, decided that if they were to have war with the Hebrews, it would be far better to fight on Hebrew soil. So they came to attack. Some of the Jews probably felt that they would have done far better if they had stayed home. Their worship provoked the attack. But the majority of them had been so revived they were willing to hazard a risk.

The devil always answers the challenge of God. When there is a spiritual stirring and the hearts of the people become repentant, the devil always responds immediately and makes a direct attack. He will not suffer good to be done without interfering. Often the people of God are too spiritually lethargic to lift up their prayers and efforts to meet the challenge of Satan, but Satan is never too listless to answer with all his strength and cunning the challenge of the people of God. This is what took place at Mizpeh.

"And the children of Israel said to Samuel, Cease not to cry unto the LORD our God for us" (vs. 8). There were two reasons for this request. In the first place, Samuel had promised to pray for them at Mizpeh. In the second place, laymen always look to the men of God for guidance and for prayer in hours of spiritual crises.

We find recorded in verse 9 how Samuel prayed unto God. Samuel offered a sucking lamb. It was a burnt offering. It was the way of access to God. When prayers are uttered in the light of the sacrifice of Christ and from under the Cross, they will reach the ear of God. There is no other access to God. Mingled with the smoke of sacrifice which ascended unto God were the prayers of Samuel. Many have been the times in history when the churches have sought God in other ways. They have been disappointed in each case. Men find peace with God only when they realize it is to be found in the righteousness of another — Christ Jesus. Luther, Bunyan, Chalmers, and countless others struggled to attain conformity to the will of God with every energy and instrument available to them, but only met with bitter disappointment until they found it in the atoning mercy of God in Christ. Prayers which are uttered in the name of Jesus Christ, who poured out His blood a libation for us, will get results.

The sacrifice of Samuel without prayer would have been but a shadow, or clouds without rain. His prayers without the sacrifice would not have prevailed. Both together teach us what great things we may expect from God in answer to our prayers made with faith in the sacrifice of Christ upon the Cross. We often pray amiss. Words in themselves are not prayers. Sighs of the heart alone are not prayers. Prayers are not prayers until they are mingled with the smoke of sacrifice. They must go up from the foot of the Cross.

"And the LORD heard him" (vs. 9). As we shall see subsequently, the Philistines were discomfited and thoroughly routed. This magnified the effectiveness of prayer and the power of God. These people were not prepared for war. They had not gathered at Mizpeh in a military camp. They were not equipped for battle. Prayer was their essential weapon. Prayer always gets results when it is uttered under proper circumstances and in the right way. Dr. J. B. Cranfill tells a true story of prayer, which took place years ago on the frontier of Texas. A fine Christian man and his wife established a prayer altar in their home. Each night the man, his wife, and two sons would gather at the hearthstone. He would read the Bible and get on his knees at a certain place on the floor in front of the fireplace and pour out his heart to God for his family. When the good man and his wife died, the young men, who had grown to be strong mature men of the West, came to make proper disposition of the estate. Neither of them were Christians. They decided to tear down the old house. With their own hands they took away the roof, the walls, and rafters, and were in the process of taking up the floor. They were taking it up plank by plank. They were large planks sawed from virgin pine trees. When they came to the plank immediately in front of the hearth, they remembered that this was the place where their godly father had knelt so many times to pray. Tears from his earnest eyes had fallen on this particular plank. They stopped and looked silently at each other for a moment. Then one said to the other, "I cannot take up this plank; I wish you would." With tears in his eyes, the other replied, "Here is where father used to pray. I cannot take up this plank." Then and there these two strong men of the West clasped each other's hands and prayed. They gave their hearts to God.[7] If your answer has not come yet, it will. God cannot fail. God answers prayer. We have an illustration in this incident of God's ability to answer prayer.

"And as Samuel was offering up the burnt offering, the Philistines drew near to battle against Israel; but the LORD thundered with a great thunder on that day upon the Philistines and discomfited them" (vs. 10). The instrument was not hail as in the time of Joshua when God discomfited the kings that marched against him (Josh. 10:11). They were not smitten with blindness as in the days of Elisha when God smote the armies of Benhadad with blindness so that they suffered defeat. But great thundering and lightning burned and scorched the hands and faces of the soldiers. In consternation they became easy prey to the sword of the Hebrews.

In their previous battle with the Philistines (4:10), the Hebrews took the ark into battle with them. This was only a symbol of the presence of God, but now they had the presence of God in reality. It made a great difference. "The

LORD thundered with a great thunder on that day upon the
Philistines, and discomfited them." In the past they had
rushed blindly into battle, led of unfit men. Now they were
led by Samuel. Then they were unconcerned about their
sins, but now they had confessed them and had a sense of
forgiveness. They had no real hope then, but now they were
confident. The truth is that the victory had been won before
a single battle contact had been made. It was won by Samuel on his knees at the holy altar.

The thunder was not necessarily supernatural.[8] It was
a natural force adapted to an answer to prayer. This often
happens in the Bible and in history. As the Philistines
climbed the heights to Mizpeh, the thunderstorm broke and
blew in their faces. They doubtlessly turned their backs to
the fierce wind and rain, and at the same time, they turned
their backs to the Hebrews. The lightning blinded them.
The thunder deafened them and confused them. The Hebrews moved with disconcerting speed upon them and
routed them. God was with the Hebrews. He was in the
thunderstorm. The thunderstorm was natural but not acci-
dental. It was the result of the laws of nature, but it was
timed by Jehovah. God made the elements. He is the Author of the laws of the universe. God did not make the laws
of the universe and go off and leave them to their course
any more than He made men and left them alone. God can
transcend nature at will and often does. This might have
been a miracle, but the chances are it was a natural storm
and timed to be of benefit to the Jews.

The battle does not always go to the strong. Napoleon
said that God is on the side of the strongest character. He
contended that the army with the most soldiers and the
best equipment would always win the victory, but Napoleon
had to eat his words at the Battle of Waterloo. Napoleon
had all of his batteries in the finest possible condition for
a great victory, but God sent a rain on the battlefield and
Napoleon was wiped off the map of the world never to
return. There is no doubt that God will bring victory to
the right side and do it every time. There are ups and downs
in life. There are momentary defeats, but in the main the

people of God will triumph. Sennacherib came against Samaria with almost two hundred thousand men, and they encamped over against the city to menace the people of God. When the destroying angel from God had finished with that formidable host that night, the next morning almost the entire army of the Assyrians was dead. The battle does not always go to the strong and to the best prepared. Might does not always win. Prayer makes a difference.

THE ACHIEVEMENTS OF THE REVIVAL

1. *It separated the people from their idols.* It brought the people back to God. It was a mighty spiritual stirring that returned the people to Jehovah.

2. *The effects of the revival guided the people in the future.* "The Philistines were subdued, and they came no more into the coast of Israel" (7:13). This statement does not signify that the Philistines were completely defeated nor that they did not threaten the Israelites, but that they were driven out of the coast country of the Israelites. "And the cities which the Philistines had taken from Israel were restored to Israel, from Ekron even unto Gath" (vs. 14). The towns which lay on the Danite frontier between these places were restored to Israel. This did not include Ekron nor Gath. Ekron was held only for a short time by the Hebrews (Judg. 1:18).

"And there was peace between Israel and the Amorites" (vs. 14). The Amorites were the most powerful enemies of Israel outside of the Philistines. The Amorites were the highlanders, in contrast with the Canaanites, who were the lowlanders.[9] The Amorites lived chiefly in the mountain areas of Judah and Ephraim (Num. 21:13). It is not known just how the revival which took place among the Hebrews affected the peace between themselves and the people who dwelled in the mountains. The mellow spirit of the Hebrews might have had some effect, and also the fear of the Amorites might have had a definite part in the desire to get along with the Hebrews. The fear of God was evidently abroad in the land.

"Then Samuel took a stone, and set it up between Miz-peh and Shen, and called the name of it Ebenezer" (I Sam. 7:12). This memorial had a twofold purpose for the people of Israel. In the first place, it glorified God. It was not for bragging purposes. They had nothing to boast about. They wanted all the earth to know and remember forever that Jehovah had delivered them from their distress at Mizpah. The glory and praise all went to God. In the second place, it was to serve as encouragement to Israel. It would be a constant source of encouragement to Israel that they had nothing to fear from without nor within if they walked by faith before God. This memorial was not a shrine. It served only as a reminder. It continually called attention to the glory of God and to His trustworthiness.

The stone was set up between Mizpeh and Shen be-cause it was here that the Philistines had defeated them twenty years before because of their sins. Now because of repentance, they had been delivered. Samuel called the name of the place Ebenezer, saying, "Hitherto hath the LORD helped us." "Hitherto" embraces the sorrows and de-feats as well as the victories. Samuel reminded the Hebrews that God often helps by letting defeat and sorrow come to them. Then again He helps by crowning His people with victory. Samuel would never forget the dark day twenty years before this when news from the battlefield brought such national and spiritual darkness. He saw the old priest Eli dead as a result of the news. Shiloh and other strong cities had been pillaged and possibly destroyed. He declared that even in sorrow God was getting us ready for victory. "Hitherto" looks forward as well as backward.[10]

On the strength of the revival Samuel was able to judge the people for many years. Samuel judged the people and when he became old, he made his sons judges (8:1). This means that the sons supplemented his work, but they did not supersede in their father's judicial office. Saul was made king of the land, but Samuel retained a civil and religious authority even after Saul had become the military leader of the people. Samuel "went from year to year in circuit

to Bethel, and Gilgal, and Mizpeh, and judged Israel in
all those places" (7:16). Bethel was about eight miles north
of Jerusalem. It was formerly the royal Canaanite city of
Luz (Gen. 28:19). Gilgal was the first station of the Israelites after the passage of the Jordan, and the place where
the men born in the wilderness were circumcised (Josh.
5:2). The first passover was celebrated here (Josh. 5:10).
Samuel also visited Mizpeh in his regular rounds of judgeship. The nation prospered under the judgeship and leadership of Samuel.

3. *The revival gave rebirth to the nation.* Samuel was
the last of the judges. Up until this time, the people had
been ruled intermittently by judges, and these judges apparently had been called of God to the task. It was strictly a
theocracy until after this revival and until Saul was crowned
king of Israel. The people desired a king, and when they
pressed upon Samuel to anoint a king, after much prayer
with God and consideration of the appeals of the people,
he consented to do so. In chapter 10, Saul is anointed king.
Revival not only leads to the birth of a nation, but it leads
to the creation of a new world order. The United States,
as a nation, in the middle of the eighteenth century received
its birth as a nation from the Colonial Revival. True revival
is not merely an emotional upheaval; it not only convicts
men of their sins and brings them back to God; but it has
even led to the birth of a nation and to the reanimation of
the civilization.

CHAPTER 4

THE REVIVAL ON MOUNT CARMEL

I Kings 18:1-46

ISRAEL BEFORE ELIJAH

1. *The political status of the nation.* Fifty-six years had passed since Jeroboam had led the revolt of the ten tribes against Rehoboam and had established the Northern Kingdom. Ahab took the throne about 919 B.C.[1] These were turbulent years for the Northern Kingdom. They had witnessed unrest from within and trouble from without. They had suffered bloodshed from within the empire and wars from without. Baasha murdered Nadab, the second king, and usurped the throne (I Kings 15:27). Baasha was a despot who pursued a merciless policy. He put to death the entire family of Jeroboam (15:29). After twenty-four years on the throne, he was succeeded by his son Elah. Elah was slain by Zimri, the captain of his chariots (16:9-10). Zimri was as despotic and cruel as Baasha. He put to death all the house of Baasha (16:11). His reign was very brief. The armies of Israel, encamped against Gibbethon, which was held by the Philistines, discontinued the siege when they heard of the actions of Zimri. Led by Omri, the army attacked Tirzah, the capital of Israel, and Zimri committed suicide by burning the palace down on himself (16:18). After several years of bitter rivalry with Tibni, Omri became king. Omri was ambitious and enterprising. He defeated the king of Moab (II Kings 3:4). He moved the capital from Tirzah to Samaria, a new city which he had built. Omri reigned twelve years and the last six years of his reign was from Samaria, the new capital. He was

succeeded at his death by Ahab, his son (I Kings 16:28). "Omri wrought evil in the eyes of the LORD, and did worse than all that were before him" (16:25). The reigns of the first six kings were turbulent with three of the six being murdered or brought to a cruel end by their usurpers.

The internal strife which existed in Israel was not the entire story. While all of this was going on, they were at war for many of these years with nations from without. War is always a disintegrating force upon the peoples of any country. Fear, hatred, and bloodshed from within and without soon brings a nation to a low moral status. If Jeroboam the son of Nebat was vile and if Omri surpassed him in evil, the worst was yet to come. Ahab laid the foundation for the ultimate destruction of the kingdom. Ahab feared the growing Syrian power centered in Damascus. He thought an alliance with Tyre on the north would guarantee protection against Syria. An alliance with Tyre was formed. This was only one of the political links in the chain which finally throttled the nation.

2. *The commercial condition of the nation.* Ahab possessed keen insight into material affairs. He determined to increase the internal prosperity of the nation. Such ambition was fine if worthy methods had been employed to accomplish the end. He was a builder of cities and palaces and a promoter of public works. He even built for himself an ivory palace (22:39). In Solomon's day, ivory was used only to build a chair of state, but Ahab decorated an entire house with it. The economy prospered in his reign. As he was instrumental in producing commercial prosperity, he violated principles which led finally to the undoing of the nation. He sought to strengthen the bonds of friendship with the thriving country of Phoenicia. Phoenicia at this time was the queen of the seas. She was a strong commercial empire. Ahab wished to profit from the maritime greatness of Phoenicia. His marriage to Jezebel, the beautiful princess of the priest-king of Phoenicia, was just one step on the ladder of commercial prosperity. Such a tie would strengthen the idolatrous trends in his nation, but religion

to him did not matter. Jeroboam had erected golden calves and perverted the Jehovistic worship, but, Ahab had no care for Jehovah at all. He used Hebrew religious terminology, but the language was wholly free from any real sense of a true and living God. Ahab may have had good qualities about him, but he had no God-centered religious convictions. He was completely void of faith in Jehovah.

3. *The religious conditions before Elijah.* Two streams of religious perversion converged upon Israel. One came from Egypt on the south, and the other, more vigorous and dangerous, came from Phoenicia on the north. These two streams of religious influence thoroughly poisoned the spiritual bloodstream of the nation. The religious perversion came from Egypt through Jeroboam. Jeroboam was a gifted man of Zereda (I Kings 11:26). Encouraged by the prophet Ahijah of Shiloh, he opposed Solomon and was exiled into Egypt (11:40). While in Egypt, he became enamored with the worship of the golden calf.

When Solomon died and Rehoboam began his reign, Jeroboam returned to Israel. The folly of Rehoboam bred dissension in the kingdom (12:16). This gave Jeroboam a chance to split off the ten northern tribes and constitute the Northern Kingdom. Religious bonds were very strong, and as the people from the Northern Kingdom would go back to Jerusalem three times a year to worship, there would be the danger of reuniting of the Northern and Southern Kingdoms. To prevent this, Jeroboam erected golden calves at Bethel and Dan (12:29), after the order of Mnevis, the sacred calf of Heliopolis, and commanded the people to worship there, saying "behold thy gods, O Israel, which brought thee up out of the land of Egypt" (12:28). The idea of the golden calves which were erected by Jeroboam, as we have already noted, was brought from Egypt. The development of this calf worship in Egypt is interesting. It was a corruption of the worship of the Most High. Men often want some visible form to symbolize God, and the first step made in this direction by the Egyptians was to worship the visible dome of the sky. Then they made the dome of the heavens anthropomorphic by erecting an exaggerated image of a woman, the source of life, in arch form to look down upon them. The next step was to erect an image of a cow in arch form to gaze upon them.[2] This type of idolatry was common during the time of the exodus and was still prevalent when Jeroboam went to Egypt. Some think that Jeroboam was trying to represent Jehovah with the figures of the calf. He may not have intended to supplant Jehovah worship with pagan rites, but six hundred years before when Aaron had permitted the Israelites to do the same thing in the wilderness, God regarded it as idolatry and sent judgment upon them. This bit of history was known to Jeroboam. It was a dangerous thing to do. It vitiated Jehovah worship and was the first step to the destruction of the nation. It was a religious perversion of the most deadly sort. Jeroboam went further than to synchronize the worship of Jehovah with the gods of Egypt at Bethel and Dan. He transferred some of the festivals to other seasons and chose priests of all the tribes of the people without restriction to the tribe of Levi (12:31). This unlawful worship became open idolatry.

The second stream of spiritual perversion came from Phoenicia. When Ahab ascended the throne in 919 B.C., he dreamed of surpassing all neighboring nations in commerce and restoring the original financial glory which the combined kingdoms had enjoyed under Solomon. His marriage to Jezebel, the daughter of Ethbaal, king of Sidon, was a premeditated step in his scheme. The young queen was a spiritual follower of Baal and Ashtaroth. Her father was a former priest of Baal who had come to the throne of Phoenicia by intrigue and murder. She had been trained by the priests of Baal. When she came to the throne of Israel, the leaders of the Baalim induced her to promote Baal worship. Baal was the sun-god. He was supposed to be the god who controlled the seasons. He was believed to send or withhold the rain. He was considered the god of might. He was called by the Greeks, the Hercules of Tyre.[3] He was the many-headed god. As the Hebrews became blinded with the concept of this false god of power, they lost sight of the God of love, mercy, holiness, and rectitude. The origin of Baal and Ashtaroth is as strange as the origin of calf-worship in Egypt. Originally, the ancestors of the Phoenicians worshiped the true God — the Most High. As their morals decayed, their conception of God degenerated. The God of heaven gave way to the dome of heaven. At this point, their concept of God differed from the Egyptians. They could see the dome of the heavens and the sun, moon, and stars. The sun, moon, and stars were deified. In their eyes the sun became the male god, Baal, and the moon became the female goddess, Ashtaroth. A great host of lesser deities represented by the stars was developed.[4] They could worship the dome of the heavens and practice sensual sins without compunction of conscience, but they could not worship the living God Most High in this fashion. Baal worship in Israel had become so entrenched that one mountain summit would have an altar to the sun, another to the moon, and another to the stars. One grove would have a shrine to the rivers and another to the rain. The summer would have still a separate shrine. There were scores of different kinds of shrines to Baal. This is why Baal was often called the "hundred-headed god."

Jezebel was in a singularly strategic position to promote her religion. She was queen of Israel and prophetess of the Baalim. She was crafty, cruel, and designing. She was revengeful and intelligent; she was beautiful. Her personality was striking. She was a much stronger character than Ahab, the king. Ahab seemed to have no religious convictions, but Jezebel had deep religious convictions and was very determined. A magnificent temple to Baalim was erected in Samaria (I Kings 16:32). Ahab erected groves to Ashtaroth also (vs. 33). Soon temples and shrines sprang up in every village and hill in Israel. Baal worship became the established religion of the land.[5] Four hundred and fifty prophets of Baal and four hundred prophets of the groves ate at the table of Jezebel. These eight hundred and fifty prophets of the false gods became the court prophets of Israel.

Baal worship was exalted above the vitiated Jehovistic worship which Jeroboam had established some sixty years before and which was prominent when Jezebel came to Israel. There were still a few in the land who held on to orthodox Jehovah worship. This number consisted mainly of a handful of faithful people and a few prophets who had been spared the sword of Jezebel by having hidden themselves in the caves and mountains of the highlands. It is probable that their position and convictions had been dreadfully weakened. Obadiah and the seven thousand who had not bowed their knee to Baal still believed in this form of Jehovah worship. Even Obadiah was content to serve amidst the abominations for the sake of expediency, but this weakened orthodoxy had little chance among the two vicious and popular religions sponsored by Jezebel and Ahab.

It had become an affront to the kingdom to worship Jehovah after the orthodox fashion. The compromising group represented by Ahab was tolerated only because Ahab was king. They were too docile to be feared, so they were permitted to carry on; but much persecution had been directed against the true worshipers of Jehovah. All the prophets had been killed except two small contingents whom Obadiah had hidden in the caves in the highlands of Israel (I Kings 18:4).

The state of spiritual degeneracy in Israel was unparalleled. Never before had the people of Israel sunk to such religious depths. Israel had completely lost her distinctive. Israel had been God's perpetual protest against polytheism, but with polytheism so firmly entrenched, Israel had lost her place. This brought the nation to the most precarious condition it had ever faced. She must forever forfeit her position among the nations and in the religious history of the world, or Jehovah must reveal Himself to her as the only living God. To save Israel now, the supremacy of God must be restored, and the nation brought back to its former allegiance to Him. It would require a remarkable leader to answer a challenge of such proportions. The glory of Israel had departed. The images of the Baalim and Ashtaroth gleamed on every side. Every hill smoked with sacrifices to the false gods, and the valleys echoed with the blasphemous shouts of pagan priests. Into the midst of this scene came Elijah as if he had been parachuted from heaven. We see nothing of him until he appears in full life as an actor from behind the stage curtains. This manner of introduction is as extraordinary as the crisis into which he came. It sets the entire stage with dramatic expectation.

THE REVIVALIST AND HIS MESSAGE

1. *The prophet Elijah.* "Elijah, the Tishbite, who was of the inhabitants of Gilead" (I Kings 17:1).

(1) As to the background of Elijah, we know very little. We know nothing of his ancestry. We know absolutely nothing about his parents. We know nothing about his home life in the mountains of Gilead, nor about his education. This expression only tells us that he was from Gilead, the rugged, rocky country east of the Jordan. This section of the country was inhabited by rugged, stern, solemn, individualistic mountain dwellers. They dwelt in rude villages and tended flocks for a livelihood.[6] We conclude that Elijah was from the mountain hamlet of Tishbe and shepherded a flock of sheep in the rough terrain of Gilead. Some deny that Tishbe was a hamlet. They say that the word means "converter" or "reformer" and that it was a title rather than a town.[7] However, though the place called Tishbe cannot be identified, the majority of writers believe the name to refer to a hamlet or village in Gilead. Elijah was hardened by the open-air life, his muscles highly developed by much climbing and manual activity. He was physically fit for the grilling task which lay ahead of him. God calls His leaders from the most unlikely places and prepares them in the most unique situations. It was in this very region that Moses received much of his training, where he led the people, taught them, and where he received the decalogue at Sinai. It was to this very region that Paul went for more than two years of study after his conversion as he compared God's new departure in Christianity to Hebrewism.

In the highlands of Gilead lived the majority of the Amorites. When the people of Israel came to Palestine, they found the Canaanites dwelling in the lowland areas and the Amorites, a local people, dwelling in the highlands. The Amorites still dwelled in the highlands. We saw in the Samuel Revival how the Amorites and the Hebrews made peace and for many years lived peacefully together. Not many of the Jews had wandered into the highland regions of Gilead, but a few families did live there. The family of Elijah was one of them.

As to the physical makeup of Elijah, it appears that he was muscular and taller than the average man.[8] He had long locks of black hair. The expression on his face was generally pensive. He had average-sized eyes, which were keen and piercing, set deep in protruding sockets like brown agates.

(2) He was a Bible student. He was familiar with the book of the law and particularly the Book of Deuteronomy. He had read, "Take heed to yourselves, that your heart be not deceived, and ye turn aside, and serve other gods, and worship them; and then the LORD's wrath be kindled against you, and he shut up the heaven, that there be no rain, and that the land yield not her fruit; and lest ye perish quickly from off the good land which the LORD giveth you" (Deut. 11:16-17). This became the text of the revival. The reports from across the Jordan revealed to him that this was exactly what had happened in Israel. He saw that they had ignored Jehovah and did not believe that this judgment would be executed. If it were not executed, the people would believe Jehovah was but a myth, and "he prayed earnestly that it might not rain" (Jas. 5:17). Prayer is faith laying hold of the Word of God. Being familiar with the teachings of the Word of God, Elijah knew that his people were in for a severe judgment. God had promised that He would shut up the windows of heaven and send a drought upon the people if they persisted in their rebellion against Him. Being familiar with the Word of God, he believed it with all of his heart.

(3) Elijah was a man of prayer. He prayed "that it might not rain." The beautiful foliage which characterized the entire land would turn brown and die. The rose and honeysuckle would bloom no more. The mountain streams and water pools would dry up. Famine would come; people and beasts alike would suffer and even die. But, was this more terrible than that the seed of Abraham, Isaac, and Jacob should turn from the living God and worship the material bodies of the heavens and bow down to piles of stone? Was this worse than to have God's people believe the propaganda of the priests of Baal that Jehovah was a myth and that Baal was a supreme being? If God ignored their accusations and open defiance of Him, would it not prove Him a myth? The prophet had to pray such a prayer. It is always better that a famine stalk the land, that people thirst, that the nation be torn limb from limb, than that the people decay spiritually; better that a depression come and twenty million people walk the streets jobless than that the people, choked on prosperity, forget God and worship at the altar of crass materialism, drinking rivers of beer and champagne rather than the wine of holy communion. Physical destruction is a smaller calamity than moral delinquency. The love of God does not shrink from inflicting such sufferings if by such judgment the plague of sin may be wiped out. It was a terrible prayer to pray, but it was necessary.

(4) Elijah was a man of faith. Elijah had no qualities which are not accessible to the ordinary man. He was a "man subject to like passions as we are" (Jas. 5:17). There was nothing particularly transcendent about Elijah. He was probably a coward in many ways. We find him later on in the story lying down upon the sands, crying unto God to take his life. But one expression in the account reveals the clear faith of the man and the quality which made for his success. When he appeared before Ahab, he said, "As the LORD God of Israel liveth" (I Kings 17:1). God may have been a mere pile of stones to the thousands of Israel, but to Elijah He was alive. He believed that God was standing in his presence, "before whom I stand" (vs. 1). Any man

who believes that God is alive, that God is present with him, and that he is a commissioned servant of God, becomes material for a miracle in God's hand. This clear faith was the source of Elijah's mystic power and courage. The prophet of fire, burning like a torch, was originally but a smoking flax. Faith made him all he was. Strength and power lie in God. Faith brings it to us.

(5) Elijah was a man of daring with a definite mission. The character of Elijah took on the nature of the rugged hills and the strength of the mountains among which he had been reared. Elijah is one of the greatest figures in the records of the kingdom of Israel. No more heroic soul ever toiled and suffered for godliness in the earth. Conscious of the presence of God, he was unafraid. His mission was twofold. His mission was to vindicate the supremacy of Jehovah and to lead Israel back to its former allegiance with God. The authority of God had been challenged by Jezebel and by the priests of Baal and Ashtaroth. The majesty of God had been insulted as they made Jehovah worship an affront to the nation. The covenant of God had been pushed aside as unimportant when Baal worship became the state religion. In order to restore the people to their original position before God, it would require an individual characterized by great daring. It would require force and grace; sweet, tender pleading would not do it. Language which the people understood must be spoken. They were crassly material, and the accents of material dialect must be spoken. Depression had to come. The fountains of water had to dry up. Thirst and hunger must stalk the land before the voice of God would be heeded. As the repeated and saddening accounts of religious disaster reached the ears of the shepherd boy in the hills of Gilead, his entire soul became sick. He could stand it no longer. With the daring of an ambassador from heaven, he appeared in the presence of the king.

2. *The message of Elijah.* Elijah spoke three times in these dramatic days. Each time his message was brief and constituted a challenge. Elijah had no pulpit; he had no recognized vantage point. He spoke his message in the open

without the surroundings of decorated walls, drapes, pipe organs, and choirs. The first one was without appointment. It was possibly delivered on the streets of Samaria or in the garden of Ahab.

(1) The first message of Elijah. He appeared before King Ahab unannounced and spoke in the name of God, "As the LORD God of Israel liveth" (I Kings 17:1). It focussed attention on Jehovah, the God Ahab had forsaken for foreign gods — the God who had long since been classified by Ahab as no more, if not less, than on a par with Baal. To Ahab, God was dead. The whole idea of God was very dim and confused in his thinking, so much so that all gods were alike and only a tool in his hands. Suddenly there stood in Ahab's presence a highlander, whose sunburned skin and shaggy raven hair formed a background for the beam of the most piercing eyes which the king had ever seen. Like a clap of thunder, his voice shocked the composure of the monarch. The content of the message was provoking. The prophet said that Israel's God, Jehovah, was alive and present. God is not off in some remote corner of the universe, but He is here. He is concerned with the people.

The second part of his message dealt with the judgment of God. "There shall not be dew nor rain" (vs. 1). It was bad enough to have no rain. Often in the dry seasons of Israel the foliage would be spared by the customary heavy dews which would fall at night, but the prophet said, "there shall not be dew nor rain." This message hit Ahab where it hurt. Ahab worshiped prosperity and had planned and toiled to build a materially strong nation. He had stopped at nothing to achieve this end. To think what would happen if the rivers should dry up, the green grass die, and cattle famish was an appalling thought. A long drought would destroy them materially. A drought that would stop the wheels of the advance of the economy was an unlikely thing, but a dreadful phenomenon to anticipate.

There was a third and vital point in the first brief message of the prophet. Elijah challenged the supremacy of

Baal over Jehovah. He was saying in substance to Ahab,
"You and your people say the many-headed Baal is the god
who controls the seasons and sends rain and dew. You have
a rain-god, a dew-god, and you say these gods send the rain
and dew and control the seasons. I shall prove that they do
not." "There shall not be dew nor rain these years, but according to my word" (vs. 1). If it rains, Baal does control the
seasons. If it does not rain, "but according to my word," then
Baal is not supreme. The prophet sought to show the king
and the people that the powers which Baal symbolized were
operative only by Jehovah. It was a dramatic challenge. The
test should have been enough to determine who is the true
and living God. Elijah was hurling thunderbolts at the
dome-god.

The prophet's mouth was opened by Another. Elijah
was bold, but it would be giving too much credit to a mere
man to fail to point out that it was God who endowed him
with the courage that opened his mouth. He spoke, not
counting the cost. The same godly courage pried open the
mouths of the early disciples when they were arrested and
brought before the Sanhedrin (Acts 4:5-14). The men of the
Reformation boldly preached what other good men had been
reluctant to say. What others for fear of personal danger had
shrunk from preaching, Luther, Calvin, Knox, and others
declared with boldness. Their mouths had been opened by
the God of Elijah.

(2)   The second brief message of Elijah. Elijah
again appeared in Samaria. When Obadiah informed Ahab
that Elijah was in the land, the king came in thunderous
haste. He bolstered his courage by swaggering up to Elijah
like a victor and saying, "Art thou he that troubleth Israel?"
This was not a sign of courage on the part of the king nor a
sense of success. It was a dead giveaway that he was cowed
and weakening. Since the time of Adam, men have tried to
lay their failures on someone else. Ahab was looking for a
scapegoat. Elijah was not the troubler; the trouble lay with
the royal house and with Israel. People often hate the minister who reveals their ruinous sins to them instead of hating

the sins which ruin them. Elijah was calling Ahab and his people back to God. Any man who vigorously and effectively calls the people back to God will meet determined opposition from the world and even from some people within the church, but it is the only solution to the world's ills. Obadiah's diplomacy will never see revival. Every minister of righteousness should be diplomatic but he should never sacrifice truth on the altar of diplomacy. Faithful ministers must, at times, be disturbers. A believing daughter may bring down upon her the wrath of an unbelieving father and mother. Often, a faithful preacher brings down upon him the wrath of an influential member of his church by fearlessly preaching a simple truth. There were many false prophets in the Scriptures, but very few true prophets. The prophet whose main achievement has been conformity and unqualified acceptance should re-examine his heart and message.

Again Elijah's message was brief and challenging. He told Ahab two things in his second appearance.

(a) He made plain who had troubled Israel (I Kings 18:18). Elijah was not the troubler just because he had been the instrument for chastising. The intemperate and unchaste life of Ahad and his people, which grew out of a departure from God, had ruined Israel.

(b) The second part of his message was an order to Ahab. "Send, and gather to me all Israel unto mount Carmel" (vs. 19). Elijah preserved the dignity of his office and character.[9] He did not cringe before the king but gave him a command from his Superior Ruler. The leader and the people must gather at Mount Carmel. All who were involved in the national sin were to be there. "So Ahab sent unto all the children of Israel, and gathered the prophets together unto mount Carmel" (vs. 20). "The prophets" referred to all the prophets of the Baalim and Ashtaroth (vs. 19). Why did the king respond so readily? He was probably desperate and had no other alternative. It would be well to remember that the Lord may have moved him to cooperate.

(3) The third challenge of the prophet. Elijah's message on Mount Carmel contained two points.

(a) "How long halt ye between two opinions" (vs. 21). The statement literally means, "How long will ye leap upon two branches?" Many of them were limping between two opinions. Down deep in their hearts they knew that they had deserted Jehovah and there was a strong pull to return to God, but it was unpopular and dangerous to be a professed follower of Jehovah. The conscience pulled from one side, and patronage from the government and ruling house from the other side. They truly limped like a crippled man between the two extremes. The main thing which had caused them to reconsider Jehovistic worship was the first challenge of Elijah and the drought. None of the great crowd present answered him when he cried, "How long halt ye between two opinions?" They were silent. An invitation to come to God is not enough. It must be accompanied by a demonstration of the power of God.

(b) Elijah made a proposition to the people. He urged the priests of Baal to build an altar and place a sacrifice on it. They were to put no fire under it but were to call upon Baal to answer by fire. The prophet would do the same thing. He would build an altar and call upon Jehovah and "the God that answereth by fire, let him be God" (vs. 24). Elijah had challenged and proved that Baal was not the god of the seasons; he could not send rain. Now he comes to challenge Baal in his last stronghold. They said Baal was the sun-god — the fire-god. Elijah's challenge proposes to prove that Baal is not even a fire-god. If he is the sun-god, he can send fire. If not, then he is a fake. If Jehovah is the God of the heavens, He can send fire. "The God that answers by fire, let him be God."

The Revival

1. *Preparation for the revival.* The preparation for the revival was twofold. The people must be prepared, as well as the preacher. The people of Israel could not understand the language of the Spirit. They could only understand the

language of the material. They had become crassly materialistic. Being forced to speak to them in their own language,
it was necessary to dry up the fountains and to cause the
heavens to become brass, bringing the people to their knees
by a terrible drought. "The words of the LORD came to
Elijah in the third year, saying, Go, shew thyself unto Ahab"
(18:1). This seems to signify that the time from Elijah's first
appearance before Ahab and his second appearance was a
little less than three years. W. M. Taylor says the "many
days" refer to the time Elijah was in Zarephath and "in the
third year" refers to the duration of the drought.[10] Our
Lord, in Luke 4:25, said the drought lasted three years and
six months, and the same figure is given by James (Jas.
5:17). In the story in I Kings we are not told how long the
drought lasted. Rev. R. G. Macintyre believes that the
drought was already in progress when Elijah appeared the
first time before Ahab. He did not announce the beginning
of the drought, but declared it to be the work of Jehovah,
and that it would not end, except according to the words
spoken by the prophet.[11]

The drought with which the land was inflicted was too
terrible for description. The sun beamed its scorching rays
upon the land. The sultry winds dried up the fields and tore
the rivulets from their beds. Every fountain in the land
ceased to bubble. Trees and shrubbery dropped their leaves
and withered. Hungry and thirsty cattle filled the whole
land with screams of terror. The brazen heavens seemed to
laugh at the sufferers and mock them in their confusion. By
the end of the three and one-half year period the people
were desperate. King Ahab was the most desperate of them
all because he had seen many of his dreams fade before the
rays of the scorching sun. This was the kind of language
the people understood.

2. *Preparation for the preacher.* As soon as Elijah had
delivered his first challenge to the king, the Lord spoke to
him and told him to "turn thee eastward, and hide thyself by
the brook Cherith" (I Kings 17:3). This was a secluded spot
east of the Jordan in the hills of Gilead. He was fenced in

by nature. Heavy underbrush and foliage of all colors were
on every side. It was a retreat for the prophet. The time
was profitably spent. He had a chance to meditate upon the
deep things of God and have fellowship with Him. Every
preacher needs a chamber. Every preacher needs a secluded
spot somewhere to which he can go occasionally to replenish
himself and get closer to God. Sermons are not built. Sermons are born. Every preacher should have all the knowledge of homiletics available to him and then he will not
have enough; but no one can learn how to preach. Sermons
are born. A man may preach magnificently and then go
away wondering how he was able to do it. The very next
time, with the same amount of study and preparation, he
may completely fail. When he wonders why he failed, let
him remember that preaching is divine, that no man can
master it. It is not an art to be mastered. We are absolutely
dependent upon God. In quiet places with God, sermons are
born in our hearts, and the Spirit gives them utterance
within the sanctuaries of the people. God had said to Elijah,
"Get thee hence, and turn thee eastward, and hide thyself
by the brook Cherith, that is before Jordan . . . and I have
commanded the ravens to feed thee there" (vss. 3-4). It is
excellent that the prophet read the entire telegram. It is
fine that he did not overlook the word "there." "I will feed
thee *there*." There were many brooks in Gilead, but there
was only one brook where the ravens would come with meat
and bread. If one is in God's will, he will be in God's place.
If he is in God's place, he will receive God's provisions, both
spiritual and physical. The ravens brought him bread and
flesh in the morning, and bread and flesh in the evening. A
little boy in Germany one cold night, after hearing his
mother read this particular account and seeing no fire in the
room and no food on the table, asked his mother if he could
open the door for the ravens to come in. He thought the
ravens must be on their way there because he and his
mother were in the same condition described in the text.
The mother really thought in her heart that to open the
door would only let more cold air in, but she permitted the

little boy to do it just to satisfy him. A fine man with a Christian heart passing by saw the door open and stopped. He went in to see why the door was open on that cold night at such an hour as that. When he was told the story, he said, "I'll be the raven." He was then, and afterwards.

Soon the brook dried up, but when Elijah saw the brook dry up, he did not begin to make plans for himself. The man of God was not in the plan-making business. It was his business to wait on God. It was his business to follow the directives of God. "And the word of the LORD came unto him, saying, Arise, get thee to Zarephath" (vss. 8-9). Zarephath, which is today called Surafend, is located in Phoenicia. For the prophet to reach Zarephath from the brook Cherith, he would have to go across at least one hundred miles of Israel. He was hated and despised by the people of Israel because the king and the priests of the false gods had led the people to believe that he was the source of their trouble. When he arrived in Zarephath, he would be in the very cradle of Baal.

The word Zarephath means a "place of the crucible," a "melting pot." At one time there may have been smelters located in the area. Often the Lord needs to melt and remake his preachers. Often the Lord takes us from the quiet place of solitude and study and brings us to some busy Zarephath. It is well to remember that Elijah obeyed the orders of God immediately. Every move of God is marked with wisdom. The man of God close to the heartbeat of the Master never questions the will of the Lord. In Zarephath he had many experiences which prepared him for the task on Mount Carmel.

"And it came to pass after many days, that the word of the LORD came to Elijah in the third year, saying, Go, shew thyself unto Ahab; and I will send rain upon the earth" (18:1). The many days here refer to the length of time which the prophet stayed in Zarephath. The majority of the scholars at this point generally agree that the stay in Zarephath must have been about two years.

We have already studied in connection with the message of the prophet his second appearance in Samaria before

Ahab, the king. We have seen how Ahab responded, and how, through the divine providence of God, he was willing to gather the people of Israel on Mount Carmel for a special assembly. This brings us to the last stage of our study in this great revival.

3. *The scene on Mount Carmel.* The contest between Baal and Jehovah, which led to the revival, took place on Carmel, the finest mountain of Palestine. It is located on the northern border of Manasseh in the western part of Palestine, immediately south of the Bay of Acre. It is about twelve miles in length and about 1,732 feet high at its loftiest peak. It extends in a southeasterly direction from the Mediterranean Sea. Along its northeastern base flows the river Kishon toward the bay. Beyond the Kishon lay the spacious plains of Esdraelon, with Mount Tabor in the distance. Due east from Carmel is the town of Nazareth. To the north stand the mountains of Lebanon and in the distant south, below Caesarea, are the plains of Sharon. Mount Carmel is ordinarily covered with thick underbrush and trees of verdant foliage. For the scene of this particular occasion, it was very likely dry and burned.

There were definitely three crowds gathered on Mount Carmel. King Ahab and the royal court, including the Phoenician priests, flaming in gorgeous vestments of purple bespangled with gold, stood near the loftiest elevation over on one side. On the other side, there was one solitary man gravely concerned, but with the light of victory on his face: a man strong in the Lord and daring in the presence of God. There was keen anticipation within his heart. That man was Elijah. To make up his group there doubtlessly were a few Hebrews scattered throughout that vast assemblage, gathered a little lower down the side of the mountain. These few people had not bowed their knee to Baal; they believed in Jehovah as the true and living God. They were in sympathy with Elijah but too fearful to stand openly with him. The third crowd was made up of the great mass of people gathered there for the spectacle. They were all over the slopes of Carmel — great multitudes of them. Some of them may have been led to conscientiously believe that they were worshiping Jehovah while they bowed themselves down before Baal. In their thinking, there may have been no difference between Jehovah and Baal.

This scene on Mount Carmel constitutes the most dramatic moment in the entire history of Israel. It was a thrilling scene. It seems too sacred to touch. It is one of those vital experiences which beggars description. No painter of any prominence has ever attempted to put it on canvas. Mendelssohn in all his genius has embodied it in song. Almost every preacher backs off and looks upon the scene in awe as his tongue clings to the roof of his mouth. The scene could never be adequately reproduced in painting, narrative, or song. It can only be attempted.

Elijah came before the assembly and challenged them to cease to limp between two opinions. Then he made the proposition that each side build an altar and call upon his God, "and the God that answereth by fire, let him be God" (vs. 24). Truth is always willing to be subjected to a practical test. When Jesus had been raised from the dead, He said to His disciples, "Behold, my hands and my feet that it is I."

The pagans erected an altar. They placed a sacrifice upon it and began to cry unto their god. Turmoil and pagan frenzy prevailed for hours as the priests of Baal pleaded with the fire-god. The entire atmosphere was electrified with dismay and heart-sickening fear, as hours passed and no answer came. Baal could not hear. He was man-made, but man could not make the synthetic god move, breathe, and answer entreaty. The most pitiful sight on earth is to see men bow down and worship a pile of stones or an image made by hand and take it for the God who made man. The writer saw this sort of thing all over Asia a few months ago. He saw hundreds of earnest people bowing down before images and shrines on high places and street intersections. On a beautiful little peninsula not far from Yokohama at Kamakura, the writer saw many hundreds of people bowing down before the big Buddha, a mighty bronze statue, and entreat it as if it were the living God. On Mount Carmel the

worshipers of Baal leaped upon the altar with the sacrifice
and begged for Baal to hear. At noon Elijah mocked them,
and they took knives and cut their flesh until the blood of
the priests flowed on the altar and upon the ground. They
continued such frenzy until the time for the evening sacrifice. Still no answer had been received.

It was time for Elijah to build his altar and to call upon
his God. Elijah spoke with a singular calmness, a holy
dignity, and a poised confidence. He went about the work
of repairing the altar and placing the sacrifice thereon with
great faith in God. The tone and manner of Elijah and the
priests of Baal stood out in bold contrast. Genuine worship
of Jehovah and the sensual fleshly orgies of the Baalim
stood side by side on Mount Carmel, and the nation had a
box-seat view of the contrast. It made a difference. It re-
called memories. It set in motion a chain of heart reactions
which proved wholesome.

Baal had been proven false. He had been beaten, but
what about Jehovah? Would He answer by fire? Could
Elijah make good his challenge? His first step was to repair
the altar (vss. 30-32). The altar became the focus of power.
In the Exodus Revival, the tent of meeting was the focus of
power. At Mizpeh, the focus of power was the altar. Here
at Mount Carmel, the altar is also the focus of power with
one difference from the Mizpeh altar. It stood here in contrast to the altars of the false gods. There stood the altar of
Baal — cold, lifeless, and without fire. It stood just as it had
been erected, except it had been stamped upon by the
frenzied and panicky worshipers. The altar of Jehovah had
always been recognized as the center of Hebrew worship.
At the altar, the people acknowledged their sinfulness before
God. At the altar, they offered up to God their sacrifices. At
the altar, they recognized God as their Saviour and De-
liverer. At the altar, they met God face to face. At the altar
God was able to deal with them and to bring reconciliation.
When Elijah had finished the altar, he had the people pour
twelve barrels of water upon it. Water ran round about the
altar and filled the trench also.

Then Elijah came near and said, "LORD God of Abraham, Isaac, and of Israel, let it be known this day that thou art God in Israel, and that I am thy servant, and that I have done all these things at thy word" (vs. 36). Elijah was not concerned with himself.nor with what would become of him. He was only concerned that the vast multitude might know that Jehovah was God in Israel. He could not bear the idea of the people thinking that Jehovah had abdicated the throne in favor of Baal, nor could he condone the idea that Jehovah and Baal could be worshiped in the same manner. He was saying in effect, so that the people could hear, "These are God's plans and not mine." Elijah continued his prayer, "Hear me, O LORD, hear me, that this people may know that thou art the LORD God, and that thou hast turned their heart back again" (vs. 37). Any preacher who will pray this prayer in the spirit of Elijah will see similar results. He will see a demonstration of the presence and power of God. When Elijah's prayer was finished, "Then the fire of the LORD fell, and consumed the burnt sacrifice, and the wood, and the stones, and the dust, and licked up the water that was in the trench" (vs. 38). This was a convicting and faith-breeding sight. This was a scene of power; a thing of wonder. This was a mighty revelation to the people. They recognized that God was in that place. When the people saw this demonstration of the power and presence of God, "they fell on their faces: and they said, The LORD, he is the God; the LORD, he is the God" (vs. 39).

When Elijah asked them, "How long halt ye between two opinions?" he was only giving an invitation. They listened in silence, but when the fire fell, they had before them a demonstration of the presence of God. They were moved. Jehovah had answered. The fire fell and they saw it. The bewildered thousands fell on their faces and shouted. The rocks of Carmel rang, and rang as if they had become silver bells. From mountain peak to mountain peak the message reverberated. The breeze from the Mediterranean swept the victory shouts across the Kishon and over the plains of Esdraelon. The distant mountainside of Tabor rang with the reverberations of victory. The whole earth shook with the vibrations of revival and spiritual victory. Every temple and shrine in Israel trembled and the throne of Baal, as far away as Phoenicia, tottered. God's people bowed before Him when they witnessed the demonstration of power. That is revival. The revival had only begun — the following chapter, I Kings 19, tells us the story of the grace of God in spiritual revival.

Chapter 5

THE REVIVAL AT NINEVEH

The Book of Jonah

The revival at Nineveh was a most remarkable, and in many instances, the most interesting revival in the Old Testament. It is the only great revival in the Old Testament which took place on foreign soil and strictly among the Gentiles. A great revival transpired in Goshen in the days of Moses, but it was largely among the Hebrews. This revival did not begin in the heart of any person. It was a strange manifestation of the Lord. Almost every revival has begun with some dedicated, praying person. But not this one. Jonah, the main human instrument in this revival, was an unwilling one. Though the revival did not begin in the human heart and was strictly of the Lord, He used a human agent. He used the preaching of Jonah. The call to repentance must come through God's appointed means.

We are only interested in the remarkable revival of spiritual religion which took place at Nineveh. This treatment will not be concerned with the historicity of the book. It is evident that the history here is not complete. The writer of Jonah was not producing a book of history, though it deals with historical fact as over against the idea of a parable. The writer was more concerned with certain evangelistic and missionary principles and achievements. The book shows that Jehovah is not a tribal God, but rather the God of all races. It teaches the susceptibleness of pagans to revealed truth. It portrays the necessity and possibility of world evangelization. It challenged the narrow, ethnic Hebrews to world vision. It would shock them out of their national prejudice and racial bigotry. It would set at the center of their hearts the wide world instead of a small neck of land along the Mediterranean Sea. The Book of Jonah and the mission for the Hebrews which it sets forth is at least eight hundred years ahead of its times, for it was not until after Pentecost that Jewish thought arose to the point of preaching the love of God to the Gentiles. After the death and resurrection of Christ and even after His commission to His disciples, it appears that the apostles did not even think of preaching to any other than the Jews. Many students of the Book of Jonah get lost in the apparent difficulties and lose sight of the purpose of the book.

The City of Nineveh

The narrative begins by stating that Nineveh was "that great city." In the second commission which God gave Jonah in chapter 3, He calls Nineveh again "that great city." The narrative also says, "now Nineveh was an exceeding great city of three days' journey" (3:2). Three days journey would have been about sixty miles.[1] This was the traditional size of the circumference of Nineveh according to Ctesias (Diodorus 2:3). Some think that the "three days" is a vague expression indicating a long time. The most acceptable explanation comes from the recent archeological discoveries made by earnest men excavating in that area. They say that the name Nineveh is used in two senses: first, to describe the city of Nineveh proper; and secondly, it includes four very large suburban areas, and possibly five. Therefore, it may be spoken of as "greater Nineveh." The sense here would be more like the idea involved in the "greater New York" area, or it would include a situation like Fort Worth-Dallas area.[2] Traces of buildings and castles, the ruins of which still remain, reveal that the circumference of the urban area was exceedingly large. John Urquhart quotes Schrader as saying that Nineveh in the days of Sargon, the father of Sennacherib, was ninety miles in circumference.[3] Nineveh proper is bound on three sides by three rivers and on the fourth by mountains. The ruins which remain reveal that it was well fortified by dams for inundating the land

and by great ramparts. The excavations show that the length of this urban area was about twenty-five English miles and the breadth, fifteen miles. This would give the greater Nineveh area a circumference of approximately eighty miles. At the time Jonah visited the city, it was the largest city in the world.[4]

The city was founded by Nimrod of the Babylonian empire (Gen. 10:11). The city was founded about 2350 B.C. and the name Nineveh was possibly compounded from the Assyrian deity, "Nin."[5] The city was located on the east banks of the Tigris some 550 miles from the mouth of the river and 250 miles north of Babylon. Since it was founded by the ruler of the Babylonian empire, it must have been originally colonized by the people of the Babylonian kingdom.

Jonah spoke of "sixscore thousand persons that cannot discern between their right hand and their left hand" (4:11). This would seem to indicate that these persons were infants of two years old and under. If this is true, then the population of the city would be no less than a million souls.[6] This figure is not incredible if we accept the "greater Nineveh" area to include the several populous suburbs and their outlying areas. The expression about their inability to discern the right hand from the left hand may have referred to their spiritual darkness; and if so, then the total population was only a hundred and twenty thousand. Since the circumference of greater Nineveh is held to be from sixty to ninety miles by classical writers, scholars, and archeological researchers, we are inclined to believe that the population was a million or more and that the expression "cannot discern between their right hand and their left hand" refers to infants and not to spiritual destitution.

The people of Nineveh were so corrupt in Jonah's day that God could not ignore it. "For their wickedness is come up before me." Their evil and wickedness had penetrated the heavens. The Ninevites were emotionally unstable. They gave way to their passions and to their desires. We learn from what the Old Testament says about them that they were politically ambitious and that they were possessed with a militaristic spirit. Their imperialism was felt across the earth. They were feared for their ruthlessness and might. The Assyrian empire had begun to distintegrate, however, by the time of Jeroboam II (II Kings 14:25).

The Ninevites were polytheists. They worshiped many gods. But their main deity was the bull-god. The image of this bull-god had a face like unto a man and wings like a bird. Paul was no doubt speaking of this particular god when he said, "And changed the glory of the uncorruptible God into an image made like to corruptible man, and to birds, and fourfooted beasts, and creeping things" (Rom. 1:23).

The Prophet — Evangelist

"Now the word of the Lord came unto Jonah the son of Amittai, saying" (1:1). The prophet Jonah was the son of Amittai. He was born in Gath-hepher and was of the tribe of Zebulun (II Kings 14:25). Gath-hepher stood on the site which is occupied by modern Mashad (Josh. 19:13), only a few miles from Nazareth. Jonah lived in the days of Jeroboam II and possibly until as late as Menaham, king of Israel. Jeroboam II began his reign about 150 years after Jeroboam I. Jonah was probably an old man when he prophesied in Nineveh. We are not sure of the dates. They could have been anywhere from 820 to 770 B.C.

God called Jonah to become an evangelist and to go to Nineveh. In God's call to Jonah we find a triad of imperatives: "arise," "go," and "cry."[7] This threefold imperative is a significant thing. It is not as harmless as may appear on the surface. These verbs point up the urgency of Jonah's commission to preach to the Gentile city. It was a matter no man could trifle with. The unquestioned authority of God runs through these imperatives like a flashing scepter from a throne. This reminds us once again that God does speak to man, and that man is capable of response.

1. *The evangelist was disobedient.* "But Jonah rose up to flee unto Tarshish from the presence of the Lord" (1:3). There are three reasons why Jonah was disobedient unto Jehovah.

(1) He was nationalistic. He was the product of his own age. The Jews had been continually oppressed by the Gentiles, regarding them as enemies of God and of Israel. The Israelites denied the capacity of the Gentiles for salvation. Jonah's mission to Nineveh was twofold. In the first place, he was to overthrow the delusion that the salvation of God was in no case for the Gentiles; and in the second place, he was sent as an instrument for the conversion of the Ninevites. Israel was to be the instrument of salvation for the nations. This idea was far from the mind of Israel at this time. Jonah was completely dedicated to the narrow conception held by his brethren. The actions of Jonah when he received his divine call to go to Nineveh and preach bear out this contention.[8] Jonah tried to run away from the presence of God and go to Tarshish. Jonah was a demonstration of the pride and fear of Israel.

No man completely escapes his age. Every man to some extent shares the faults of his generation. Chrysostom was possibly the greatest preacher of all times, and yet he, too, was affected in many respects by the age in which he lived. He used long, drawn-out descriptions, piled up imagery, and often tires us with his excessiveness. Luther never got away from many of the errors of his age. He believed in the union of church and state and persecuted those who did not believe as he. Great old Increase Mather was not completely free from the superstitions of his time He believed in witchcraft at the turn of the eighteenth century.

(2) Jonah was disobedient largely because of his unconcern for the lost thousands of Nineveh. Nineveh was engulfed in spiritual darkness and was threatened by destruction, but Jonah did not care. Jonah's unconcern for the Gentiles was a tragedy. The unconcern of thousands of Christians today for the lost all around them is an equal tragedy. Every Christian knows that there is an eternal destiny of darkness and defeat for the lost and that sinners are doomed, yet there is an appalling unconcern in the hearts of Christians. We may stand off at a distance and condemn Jonah for his unconcern, and yet we apparently are just as

unconcerned as Jonah and his generation. We sin against more light than Jonah because Christ had not come to earth in Jonah's day. He had not died upon the Cross. He had not been raised from the dead. He had not ascended into glory. He had not sent His Holy Spirit. He had not given His churches in Jonah's day.

The prophet tried to escape "the presence of the Lord." He was withdrawing himself from the services of Jehovah, the God of Israel. He thought God was localized. He didn't seem to realize that God was everywhere and that God was the God of all the peoples of the earth.

(3) There is a third reason why the prophet was disobedient. He actually feared that the sinful city would hear and repent, and that the compassionate God would refrain from destroying them. The prophet wanted Nineveh destroyed. He had no desire to see them repent (4:1).

2. *The disobedient evangelist is afflicted.* "But the LORD sent out a great wind (1:4). It literally means that the Lord "threw" a great wind into the sea. God sent the wind to create a crisis for the prophet. God often sends crises upon His people. The mariners became afraid and began to call upon their gods. They entreated every one aboard the ship to call upon his god. But Jonah "was gone down into the sides of the ship; and he lay, and was fast asleep (1:5). While the mariners threw the cargo into the sea and struggled hard to save the ship, Jonah slept. The angry waves, churned by fierce winds, did not get through to his soul. A hounding conscience, no doubt, coupled with fatigue, had driven Jonah to the escape of a deep sleep. Nothing is more exhausting than the burden of a guilty conscience. He was in the refuge of deep sleep when the mariners wakened him. Jerome suggests the very opposite to this view. He said that Jonah was so peaceful of mind and so undisturbed that he could sleep while others feared.[9] His actions, it is held, reveal careless self-security. Regardless of which view is correct, we know that no one sleeps more soundly than a backslidden Christian, and no one is more oblivious to the cry of a dying world. The shipmaster was quite disturbed that Jonah could sleep in such an hour of threatening storm.

The mariners felt that someone aboard the ship was responsible for the turbulence. They cast lots and the lot fell upon Jonah. When they probed Jonah, he confessed that he was guilty. He told them that he was a Hebrew and that he feared "the LORD, the God of heaven." When they inquired of him as to what they should do, he said to them, "Take me up, and cast me forth into the sea; so shall the sea be calm unto you" (1:12). The sailors were scrupulously fair in the trial of Jonah and in the execution of the verdict. They did everything within their power to keep from throwing Jonah into the sea. They "rowed hard," they literally "digged." They prayed unto their gods and then they prayed unto Jehovah, the God of Jonah. Finally they became submissive to the wishes of God. With great reluctance they cast Jonah into the sea; "and the sea ceased from her raging" (1:15).

The revival which swept Ninevah actually began at sea among these pagan sailors. They saw that God was just. They saw that He was to be obeyed. His favorites had no dispensation to do as they pleased. They saw that God would even send judgment upon His prophets when they were disobedient to Him. "Then the men feared the LORD exceedingly, and offered a sacrifice unto the LORD, and made vows" (1:16). These pagan sailors did three things: first, they feared God. In the beginning the fear was for their lives. They were nothing more than afraid; but when they saw how God quieted the storm, then they feared Him in their hearts. It was then that they began to exercise reverence toward Jehovah. In the second place, they offered a sacrifice unto the Lord. This sacrifice, of whatever nature it might have been, was certainly a sin offering unto Him as well as a thank offering. And in the third place, they made vows. They pledged unto Him. No doubt they pledged to Him their lives, their loyalty, and their allegiance.

The prophet-evangelist was given a strange passage. "The LORD had prepared a great fish" (1:17). The verb here for prepared means "ordained" or "counted" or "numbered" and is not usually used in case of a special creation on the spot. The majority of the scholars think that the fish was a particular fish, i.e., one for providential use.[10] It may mean, therefore, that God determined that a particular fish swallow Jonah. However, the usage of the verb "to prepare" in this context would certainly indicate that it could have been a special preparation. The same verb is used in chapter 4, verse 6, to describe the special creation of *gīgāyōn*, and in verse 7 the preparation of a worm, and in verse 8 the preparation of a wind. It is certain from the description of the *gīgāyōn* in chapter 4 that it did not exist before Jonah arrived, and that it was a special creation. It is just as evident that the worm which destroyed the gourd vine was also a special preparation, though the same verb was used to describe these preparations which was used to describe the preparation of the fish. At any rate, the repetition of the verb in these accounts is very effective. Certainly God ordains the development of history. It is not incredible to believe that if God made the world and all creation in it in the first place, that He could have made a fish capable of swallowing a man and carrying him to a distant shore without taking his life. There is a likelihood that the fish already existed and God merely "numbered" it for the task. To cling strictly to this view would be to depend altogether on natural history for proof, and would by-pass the miraculous. There is no point in straining at this particular verb because the miraculous permeates this entire account.

The fact that Jonah was able to live in the fish for three days does not stagger the faith of one who believes in a miracle-working God. If man is able to create a pressurized compartment in an airplane, so that one may safely ride twenty-five thousand feet high, and if man is capable of building a submarine in which men may ride in the depth of the sea underneath the icy masses of the north with safety, then is it incredible to believe that the God who made man could also make a fish with a pressurized compartment in his stomach in which a man may live for at least three days? Man is not greater than God. All things are possible with God. An element of the supernatural has been connected with every revival which has been recorded in history. This one is no exception.

3. *The evangelist prayed* (2:1-9). He prayed to God from whom he had tried to escape. He was repentant and out of a changed heart he cried unto "his God." It is the prayer of a man well versed in the Holy Scripture.[11] He used many passages from the Psalms which suited his petition better than his own words. "Out of the belly of hell cried I" is a poetic expression which refers to the danger of death rather than to the belly of the fish. He was praying from the belly of the fish, but his concern was with the nearness of death. The sailors had been the instruments of judgment which God used, and Jonah recognized this truth in his prayer when he said, "For thou hadst cast me into the deep." His prayer reached unto God, for God heard his voice. He expressed in his prayer the bitterness of being "out of thy sight." He was running away from the sight of God; but when he got a real taste of what it meant to be out of the sight of God, it literally shook him. Then he longed for the presence of God. "I will look again toward thy holy temple" was a profession of faith that God would deliver him. Looking toward the temple was a symbol of prayer. When the prophet reached the stage of real repentance, he said, "I will sacrifice unto thee . . . I will pay that I have vowed" (2:9). The actions of the pagan sailors were the same as that of the penitent prophet when revival began in their hearts. Both the sailors and the prophet made sacrifices of some sort unto God and pledged allegiance. Jonah could only offer a sacrifice "unto thee with the voice of thanksgiving." The revival had broken out in two places: on the ship among the sailors and under the sea in Jonah's heart. It reached Nineveh. The Ninevites responded, as we shall see subsequently, in almost the same manner as the sailors and the prophet.

4. *The repentant prophet was delivered.* "And the LORD spake unto the fish, and it vomited out Jonah upon the dry land" (2:10). The fish was probably as happy to get rid of Jonah as Jonah was to be vomited up. As soon as Jonah's feet had touched dry land, the Lord appeared unto him again with the second commission, saying, "Arise, go unto

Nineveh, that great city, and preach unto it the preaching that I bid thee" (3:2).

The Preaching of Jonah

"Preaching that I bid thee" is good preaching, irrespective of the results. Jonah preached what God told him to preach. Dr. C. E. Matthews says, "that kind of sermon is great regardless of results."

1. *Jonah warned the people.* "Yet forty days, and Nineveh shall be overthrown" (3:4). He let the people know their plight. He warned them that they were in the path of danger. Every preacher must let that indifferent sinner who sits and listens to him know one thing for sure — unless he turns, he will spend eternity in hell. There are those who say there is no point in scaring people either to accept Christ or shun the awful destiny of sin. They claim that they believe in the gospel of love, not the gospel of a crisis. It may be well to remember that Christianity is a crisis religion, and that the Gospel preached by Christ was both love and crisis. It is just as imperative today that we bring people face to face with the stern realities of life and that we acquaint them with the truth of the certain judgments of God. It is just as vital that this be done now as it was in the days of Jonah. Jonah went everywhere preaching one thing, "Yet forty days and Nineveh shall be overthrown." The people must be brought face to face with the ruin of ·sin. They must be convicted. The Holy Spirit convicts of sin but He uses the truth as an instrument for His work. The truth must be proclaimed by the preacher. Preaching must often rebuke and reprove.

Jonah may or may not have been known to Nineveh. It was not necessary that the prophet have a name among them. His converting power came solely from God. It is likely that he gave his experience aboard the ship and in the fish. He may have introduced his sermon with an account of the strange passage. This could very well have been responsible for the sudden interest of the people. It was the convicting power of God and the living truth, however, that caused repentance. Jonah's strange approach to the city and the feeling of impending doom which became prevalent all over the city, possibly created a ripe situation for God to do His work. Jonah capitalized on the situation. He told them that they would be destroyed within forty days. He brought them face to face with doom. His cries were filled with the thunderclaps of judgment. He did it not to frighten them, but God did it to paralyze them with awful conviction. We may criticize Elijah, Jonah, Jonathan Edwards, and Charles Grandison Finney for the fierce warnings which they hurled at their congregations, but do not forget that they saw great and gratifying results. For the most part, the result in each case was wholesome. Excitement will accompany revival. With it will inevitably come dangerous excesses, but the abnormalities may be curbed by wise guidance. To warn the people is essential for revival.

2. *Jonah preached repentance.* This is not positively stated in the text, but it is implied in the words and actions of the Ninevites. The king and his nobles joined in the exhortation by means of a decree, saying, "Let them turn every one from his evil way, and from the violence that is in their hands" (3:8). God granted repentance to the entire city. Repentance of the Gentiles is nowhere else in the Old Testament as plainly illustrated.[12] George Adam Smith says that this lifts the Book of Jonah to equal rank with the second part of Isaiah and nearest of all the prophets to the New Testament.[13]

3. *The prophet preached that "Salvation is of the* LORD*"* (2:9). He came to this sweeping realization in the belly of the fish and no doubt used the great gospel truth in his exhortation. "Salvation is of the LORD" means that it is not by ceremony; it is not of man, nor by works, but it comes strictly from God. It is not a cultural and educational process, but an act of God. The same great gospel truth, which is used by evangelists today, was used nearly eight hundred years before Christ by Jonah. "Salvation is of the LORD." This expression had a fuller meaning to the Ninevites. It meant that salvation was not of Dagon nor of any of their

accepted deities. This uncompromising preachment ruled out the possibility of salvation from anyone but Jehovah.

THE REVIVAL

This revival began at the top. As a rule, revival begins with the ordinary people and then moves up to all levels. There have been few exceptions. The revival at Nineveh and the one held under Hezekiah were, for the most part, exceptions. The people who first believed in Nineveh seem to have been the leaders, for the account reads, "So the people of Nineveh believed God, and proclaimed a fast" (3:5). The next sentence describes the actions of the king. He laid off his kingly robe and sat in sackcloth and ashes, proclaiming and publishing a decree throughout the land that all should turn from their evil.

1. *They believed God* (3:5). The preaching of Jonah caused them to believe. "Faith cometh by hearing, and hearing by the word of God" (Rom. 10:17). Their faith was in direct response to the prophet's announcement of impending doom. The response was "from the greatest of them even to the least of them" (3:5). It was the response of the total population of the city. It included the old and the young, and from the king on the throne to the common man in the market place. The results were unparalleled. Never in all history was there such a revival. We do not know the number of converts. But it was likely between eight hundred thousand and a million. Never before or since has such an evangelistic phenomenon been recorded. This fact causes many to argue that the book is poetic and fictional.[14] However, it has the very opposite effect for the majority of Christians because this great account of the glorious revival challenges the faith of the people of God. Only two other revivals are to be classified with this one, and they do not begin to approximate it. The Pentecost experience was greater in prominence and was more far reaching, but it was not any more spectacular. It is reported that, as a result of Charles Grandison Finney's revival in Rochester, New York, in 1830, between ninety and a hundred thousand people actually were converted and united

with the churches of the entire area. But the territory included in the count was far wider than at Nineveh, for Rochester was a comparatively small city in 1830.

2. *They cried mightily unto God and fasted* (3:8). Men and beasts, it seems, joined in the cry.[15] A great wailing rent the air. We do not know how long they cried unto God. We find here the waking-up out of careless security. Their sins had undermined them, and they were on the verge of national catastrophe. They were willing to forsake their evil ways and to trust in Jehovah. This lamentation which resulted in great revival looms more remarkable when we realize that they had known almost nothing above Jehovistic worship. They had been confused all their lives by blinding polytheism. Here in the face of doom they were like little helpless children wailing after the God of Israel.

3. *God forgave them* (3:10). When they turned from their evil and cried mightily unto Jehovah, He had mercy on them. He extended His grace to them. God always has mercy upon the penitent who confesses and mourns over his sins with a desire to change. A great change came over the people at Nineveh. The revival was so genuine that the prophet was displeased at the phenomenal results.

The effects of revival among the pagans and the Jews in the Old Testament stand in contrast here. On Carmel, the Hebrews fell upon their faces and confessed, "the LORD he is God." When revival came to Jerusalem under Hezekiah, the people were glad and sang praises and rejoiced. But here in Nineveh there was much wild and frenzied weeping, but nothing is said of a deep joy. We believe that great gladness did prevail, but the record does not declare it. And joy certainly was not as marked in Nineveh as in the revivals among the Jews, who were no strangers to revealed religion.

CHAPTER 6

THE REVIVAL UNDER ASA

II Chronicles 15

Knowledge of the revival under Asa is of great value to the modern age because of its unique features. Many of the methods used in this revival are common to all revivals, but some of the measures employed are radically different. The decline of the revival under Asa points up grave dangers of which every generation should be aware. This revival writes a record on both sides of the ledger, with which the students of historical evangelism must be acquainted.

BACKGROUND OF THE REVIVAL

1. *A period of reformation preceded the revival.* It was not a time of religious decline. The two kings before Asa had neglected spiritual religion, and the people were in a state of religious destitution; but Asa began his reign by reversing the state policy and instituting ecclesiastical reform.[1] This reform movement by the king lasted fifteen years before the revival began. He took away the altars of the foreign gods and put forth an effort to remove the high places (II Chron. 14:3). The "high places" had become popular for sacrifice among the Israelites in the reign of Solomon before the temple was built (I Kings 3:2). Offering sacrifices on high places or on altars in the open was at first acceptable. Abraham built an altar at the spot where the Lord appeared unto him (Gen. 12:7). Later he left there and went to a mountain east of Bethel. "And there he builded an altar unto the Lord" (Gen. 12:8). The practice in itself was not evil. But after the erection of the

temple as a place of divine worship, the Israelites were prohibited the use of "high places" for worship (Deut. 12:11-14). High places became identified with idolatry. But the custom of Jehovahistic worship at open, elevated altars had become so entrenched in the worship of God's people that it was very difficult to stamp out. Abraham practiced it. Solomon permitted it until the house of worship was completed, and many of the old-timers ignored the pentateuchal prohibition. Asa never did stamp it completely out of the practice of Jehovah worshipers (II Chron. 15:17). Hezekiah, a hundred and seventy years later, was still struggling with the problem of "high places" (II Chron. 28:4). All "high places" were not idolatry. Some of this type of worship was carried on by independent, non-conforming Jehovah worshipers; but by this practice they were setting a dangerous example.

Asa had commanded Judah to seek the Lord God of their fathers. They were to observe the law and practice it. They were to follow the commandments of Jehovah. The first part of his reign saw many wholesome reforms. Since it was not a period of religious decline, the revival under Asa is different from most other revivals. Revival is generally preceded by spiritual dearth and religious chaos. This revival is an exception.

2. *It was a time of prosperity.* Along with religious reform and the raising of moral ideals came physical prosperity. It was not a time of depression. Financial despair did not cause the people to turn to God. They had plenty, and their economy was fairly secure.

A great building program was vigorously prosecuted (II Chron. 14:6-7). Great physical improvements in hundreds of towns and cities took place. New cities were built. The cities, old and new, were repaired and fortified. An unprecedented program of public works was successfully promoted. As a rule, prosperity follows in the wake of revival. This has been true of most revivals and was the case in all the revivals in America. Roger Babson points out that the cycles of prosperity always parallel spiritual revival.

Prosperity never fails to follow immediately upon spiritual awakening. The Asa Revival is an exception to this rule. Trouble is generally necessary to cause people to turn to God. As a rule men seek God only when their physical needs are extreme. This has been the case so many times in history that we often think revival cannot come apart from hardships and depression. The revival under Asa refutes this idea. This particular revival reminds us that God's spirit can work any time and under any circumstance.

Leaders with foresight and wisdom reigned. It was a time of peace. War is generally a sign of weakness. Weak leaders go to war, but strong leaders fight only when war is thrust upon them. In his latter years, Asa forsook some of the principles which made him and thereby lost ground. When he was tired and sick, his judgment disintegrated and some of his decisions were faulty. But in the main, he did good all his life.

3. *National victory formed part of the background for the revival* (II Chron. 14:9-15). While Asa built cities and grew a healthy economy, he also provided military protection. Designing neighbors are always ready to pluck ripe plums left unguarded. Asa knew when his nation prospered that some formidable ruler from without would seek to pillage them. He built an army of a little better than a half million (vs. 8). It was an army for protection. It was wisdom to provide such safeguard. Zerah from Ethopia led an army of a million against the army of Asa. Asa's forces engaged them in battle in the valley of Zephathah at Mareshah. Asa's army, only half as large, completely routed the Ethiopians (vs. 13). But the king knew that the victory was not altogether by military stratagem. "Asa cried unto the LORD his God, and said, LORD, it is nothing with thee to help, whether with many, or with them that have no power: help us, O LORD our God; for we rest on thee, and in thy name we go against this multitude. O LORD, thou art our God; let no man prevail against thee" (vs. 11).

Asa's forces returned to Jerusalem with great abundance of spoil and flushed with the spirit of victory. Here again the revival of Asa, which immediately followed, was an exception. Revival does not usually come to a people intoxicated with victory in war. It did, however, on this occasion.

THE ORIGIN OF THE REVIVAL

1. *The prayer of the king* (vs.'11). The revival began in the heart of the king. He had instituted wholesome reforms, but reformation is not revival. Reform may begin with enforcing the law and with righteous acts; but revival begins in the heart, and usually in the heart of one person. On the battlefield the king faced tremendous odds. He felt the need of the help of a personal God. "He cried." These were not mere words. Prayer was the cry of the heart. It was direct. He spoke to God out of urgency. There are two facts to reflect upon in the prayer:

(1) He confessed the limitless power of God. He said, "it is nothing with thee to help, whether with many, or with them that have no power" (vs. 11). The strength of man is nothing on either side. God's power is the determining factor. To recognize this truth is to stand in the realm of the miraculous. The prayer of Asa in battle showed a remarkable faith. He believed that God could make the fewer superior to the more numerous.[2] This kind of faith put foundation under his goodness and gave God a basis of operation in Asa's life.

(2) He placed the responsibility for victory or defeat clearly on God. "Thou art our God; let no man prevail against thee" (vs. 11). When victory came, he gave God the credit. If the responsibility for victory rests on God — and it does — let God have sole credit when victory comes. Asa exercised faith, and God honored it. His soldiers may have been flushed by victory but the king was humbled. He knew it was of God.

2. *The second contributing factor to the origin of the revival was a message of Azariah.* The message was timely. "He (Azariah) went out to meet Asa" (15:2). Great victories on the battlefield are almost always celebrated with wild frenzy accompanied by drink and hilarious frivolity.

This national victory was celebrated by giving attention to a serious message from God. The impulses which had gripped the king's heart on the battlefield could have been relaxed by deafening shouts of praise for him, followed by rounds of wild national celebration. The firm, sobering plea of the prophet guarded and preserved the spiritual impressions of the king. The sermon of Azariah curbed somewhat the fleshly demonstrations stirred by victory. The message of the prophet contained three points: a challenge, a review of revival history, and an admonition.

(1) He challenged the king and the nation to seek the Lord (vs. 2). He did not congratulate Asa on splendid victory, nor did he indulge in flattery to court princely favor. His message was a prophetic warning and a word of encouragement to stimulate vision and courage. Many helpful reforms had been instituted. The religious deeds had helped. The people were in a fine frame of mind, and God had blessed them with victory. But that was not enough. The prophet urged them to seek a deeper knowledge and fellowship with God. He reminded them that the Lord had been with them; now would they be with the Lord. Now was the time to find Him. He urged upon them a personal experience with God. "If ye will seek him, he will be found of you" (vs. 2).

(2) He reviewed the history of God's people in the time of the judges. The rule of the judges was spasmodic. The work of the Lord under them was unorganized, and the cities were without military protection. There was almost no security of life or property, and yet the people had sought for God and found Him.[3] The Book of Judges records the intermittent revivals which came each time when God's people cried unto Him. "And the children of Israel cried unto the LORD, saying, We have sinned against thee" (Judg. 10:10). God sent Jephthah to deliver them from the oppressors. When they were under the heel of the king of Mesopotamia, they cried unto the Lord, and the Lord raised up Othniel as saviour. They were in bondage to Moab eighteen years, and when they cried unto the Lord, He gave Ehud to save them. In a similar bondage

they repented, and God sent Deborah and Barak to deliver them. They were freed from the Midianite bondage by Gideon.

Azariah reasons with Asa and the people that if God sent revival to the people in times of weakness, He could surely send real revival to a strong and courageous people. He reminded Asa that the throne was now firmly established and that the influence of the royal court was on the side of God. Preachers like himself had liberty to preach, and the priests had freedom and facilities to sacrifice. The Lord could be found, and revival could surely come to Judah.

(3) He admonished Asa to be strong. This may appear to be rather strange language to be directed to a conqueror. Asa had just returned from victory over an army of a million soldiers. Could this advice be irrelevant? The courage of the battlefield is one thing, but the courage to face and crush moral evil and theological fallacy is another. There was sin in his own household.[4] His own queen mother was an idolatress (15:16). It requires a firm courage to squarely face sin in the home and church. It is easier to confront spears and guns than sin in high places. Asa needed purpose and courage. This timely message of the son of Oded accomplished this purpose. When Asa heard the words of the prophet, he took courage. The prophet urged the king to count the cost. It always costs to lead a nation in a total revival. The prophet and the king were aware of the magnitude of the task before them. The king had restored national prosperity and had built a powerful military machine, but his most difficult task lay ahead of him. It would be a greater challenge to create national righteousness than to build mighty armies.[5] Asa needed the insight and encouragement of the prophet. When he heard the message, new courage was born in his heart.

THE RETURN TO GOD

1. *Idols were put away.* That which took place from this point on is revival, not reformation. The purpose of

Asa had changed. He was no longer merely concerned with religious reform. He purposed to see his nation experience spiritual power. All idols, and not merely the most offensive, must go. All idolatry must cease. Asa had been so openly blessed that the people saw that God was with him. There was still room, however, for great improvement. Some evils were still tolerated, but they were now in the process of be-· ing pulled up by the roots. Asa's dedication is seen in his total attitude toward all idolatry and all idolaters. Asa had the courage to treat his own queen mother and her idolatrous practices in the same manner with which he dealt with the subjects of his kingdom. This sort of government was wholesome for the nation. It requires great strength to stand against evil in all places. Anyone can easily become vociferous about the evil practices of his enemies. But it requires holy boldness to move against evils in one's own bailiwick.

2. *He renewed the altar of the Lord.* The altar here is designated as "the altar . . . that was before the porch of the LORD" (vs. 8). This distinguishes between the true altar of the Lord and the altars in "high places." (vs. 17). This denotes a return to spiritual religion. To break in pieces the idols and take "away the altars of the strange gods" (14:3) was merely a negative approach and an effort at reform. But to renew the altar to Jehovah was a positive and vital act. The building of the altar signified a resumption of sacrifices. To the altar the people brought their sacrifices, and the sacrifices had a peculiar meaning for the Hebrews.

3. *The Feast of Weeks was always held in the third month, fifty days after the Passover* (Deut. 16.9). All the males of the Hebrews appeared before God three times each year: "in the feast of unleavened bread, in the feast of weeks, and in the feast of the tabernacles" (Deut. 16:16). Every man gave gifts, according to the blessings of the Lord. At the Feast of Weeks they made freewill offerings and rejoiced before the Lord. It was a time of rejoicing. The Feast of Weeks came providentially for this revival, for the hearts of the people were more susceptible

during the great spiritual convocations. The people were specially prepared for this convocation. They had just been exalted by military victory. The message of the prophet Azariah had wielded their minds into a serious frame, challenging them to be strong and seek God with their whole heart. The altar of the Lord had been repaired. The mighty annual festival came at exactly the proper time to fan the flame into revival proportions. Almost all the great revivals of the Old Testament came during the religious festivals. This convocation did not give rise to the revival, but it was definitely a promotional method for the revival. The Judean subjects were joined by great numbers of Israelites who responded to the spirit which prevailed in Judah and came to observe the Feast of Weeks. The people of Judah were not suspicious of their brethren from Israel, nor did they view them as prodigals. Revival melts prejudices and dissolves national differences.

4. *The people "entered into a covenant to seek the* Lord *God of their fathers with all their heart and with all their soul"* (15:12). They made vocal their solemn covenant. "And they sware unto the Lord with a loud voice, and with shouting, and with trumpets" (vs. 14). The observance of the covenant was not a matter of individual loyalty but was to be guarded and enforced by the community.[6] All offenders would be punished. All who would not seek the Lord were to be put to death. This was a stern measure and can only be understood in the light of Hebrew history. The type of apostasy involved here is more than an ecclesiastical offense. It included patriotism and morality. Jehovah worship was natural and correct for those who had been affected by a return to God with the whole heart. But for those who came along because of the decree of the king, it was different. Their hearts were not in it, and for them it was not revival. It was enforced conformity. It would not be correct to say, however, that Asa enforced a religious revolution. Under his leadership and under the preaching of Azariah, a spiritual awakening transpired. While coercion is never proper in spiritual revival,

it is only fair to say that the type of thing described in verse 13 must not be understood in the light of modern religious prejudice and coercion. The apparent harshness in verse 13 is a figurative way of insisting that the entire community must unitedly help stamp out disintegrating theology.[7] Some of the revivals of the Old Testament, such as the revival under Hezekiah, had little, if any, emphasis on theology, but this awakening vigorously opposed bad theology. The beliefs of men were considered important. Asa and his compatriots held that poison theology would provide the foundation for religious bankruptcy. They tried vigorously to obliterate evil theology. There prevailed among the people a naive assumption that men could take liberties with divine instructions and spiritual worship. Asa had to counter this idea with both the negative and the positive approach.

RESULTS OF THE REVIVAL

1. *An inevitable effect of the revival was joy.* Great joy always comes to the people in time of revival. Sin is a tyrant in all forms. It oppresses and torments its victims. When men are delivered from the rule of sin, they naturally rejoice. Freedom is one of the strongest urges of men. When the power of sin is broken and spiritual liberty prevails, men rejoice. Peace is a blessed possession. Peace with God, the Creator, is a healing experience. It is difficult to express the feeling that goes through the soul of an individual when he is redeemed. Joy and gladness is the only possible way of expressing this sense of forgiveness and peace. When men debate a matter in their minds and arrive at a conclusion, publicly casting off what they knew all along was wrong, there comes a great sense of relief. To break with what one knows is evil brings peace of mind and joy of soul. To be right with God and right with one's fellow man produces great joy.

2. *They found the Lord.* "And he was found of them" (vs. 15). They had sought for him "with their whole desire." They had made subordinate every ambition and

desire. All feelings, longings, and urges had been set aside or made secondary. The desire to know God and to be reconciled to Him took precedence over everything else. Personal ambitions, physical security, fleshly lusts had been relegated to their proper place. The prophet Azariah had told them "if ye will seek him, he will be found of you" (vs. 2). No doubt the prophet gave them instructions on how to seek the Lord. The law said, "if . . . thou shalt seek the LORD thy God, thou shalt find him, if thou seek him with all thy heart and with all thy soul" (Deut. 4:29). It is likely that Azariah used and expounded this law to them. We can conclude from this that any people who seek the Lord will find Him. Jeremiah pleaded with his generation nearly three hundred years later. "And ye shall seek me, and find me, when ye shall search for me with all your heart" (Jer. 29:13). It is apparent from the story, however, that all did not find the Lord. Some did not seek Him. The mother of Asa persisted in her idolatry. She refused to give up the gods of the grove and was removed from being queen (vs. 16). While only a few in Judah like Maachah, Asa's mother, did not find the Lord, far greater numbers in the Northern Kingdom remained in idolatry (vs. 17). Some will not be moved regardless of the blessings of God upon thousands around them. They remain cold and blind to the presence of God. This is one of the tragedies of life. It is tragic that when revival fires burn in an area, some will remain aloof.

3. *God gave peace to the nation.* "The LORD gave them rest round about" (vs. 15). This was a fulfillment of the promise given by the prophet in verse 2. There was no more war during the reign of Asa until the thirty-fifth year (vs. 19). This must be qualified by I Kings 15:16-17 to simply mean that nothing of a really serious nature happened until the thirty-fifth year of his reign. Baasha of Israel continually threatened the boundaries of Asa's kingdom, and there were, according to the records, disturbances between the two kingdoms during the reigns of Baasha and Asa.

THE DECLINE OF ASA'S REIGN

Asa did three things which marked a period of decline. He allied himself with Ben-hadad, the pagan king of Syria; he imprisoned the prophet Hanani; and he went to physicians when he became ill. Two of these charges would not be leveled against king or reformer today. It would be considered smart to form an alliance with a strong neighboring empire today, if that empire was in position to strengthen the national standing of the ally. It would be considered a sign of an eccentric in this day to refrain from receiving the best medical advice available. In the light of our times only one of the charges is really serious. He resented the message of the prophet Hanani and threw him into prison. Hanani's speech reminded the king that he had misplaced his faith. When his faith was in Jehovah, he crushed an immense army of Ethiopians. But recently he had placed his faith in a pagan king to help him against a comparatively weak opponent. He reminded him that Jehovah was still looking all over the land for men who would trust Him. The same God who blessed him against Zerah could have given him victory over Israel and the Syrians. He told the king rather bluntly that he had played the fool. Asa resented this very strongly and put the prophet in the prison house. In the prison house the body of the offender was often forced into an unnatural twisted position. The victim was probably bent double with hands and feet fastened securely.[8] It was as humiliating as painful. To be placed in the prison house was to lose face. It appeared in this case that many of the king's subjects deeply resented the treatment of the prophet and made a stir over it. The king immediately retaliated by crushing them. The same people whom he had led in revival twenty years earlier, he now persecuted. Authority and soft living often contribute to the loss of humility and sound judgment. By this time the revival had receded, but it is fair to say that twenty years of revival in troublesome times is very good.

A policy of diplomacy, which may be considered very

wise in our day, might have been considered very foolish in the day of Asa. Alliances with pagan kings were frowned upon by the Lord. They had too many dangerous implications, and in almost every case God's people were hindered by such foreign alliances.

Asa became very ill in the thirty-ninth year of his reign (16:12). He went to physicians rather than to the Lord. Physicians are condemned, at least by implication here.[9] The prophets and priests were generally the physicians of the Hebrews (I Kings 17:17-24, II Kings 20:1). The physicians mentioned here were very likely idolatrous medicine men who used incantations and adjurations. To read modern conceptions into ancient realities would be a mistake. Our modern conception of medical science is a far cry from the practice of "physicians" in Judah when Asa was sick. When Asa went to physicians, he revealed the degree to which his former loyalty had disintegrated. When men turn to God, revival is born; and when they turn from God, revival dies.

Chapter 7

THE REVIVAL LED BY HEZEKIAH

II Chronicles 29:1-36; 30:1-27; 31:1-21

A great revival developed under the leadership of Hezekiah. It sprang up among a people whose morals had decayed and whose hopes were dim. They were overrun by their neighbors, and they were humanly incapable of throwing off the reproach. Poverty and lack of national courage so characterized them that no one dreamed that strength of character could come to such people. The revival came as suddenly as a tornado and spread over the land with the speed of a forest fire. To appreciate this amazingly spiritual phenomenon, it will be necessary to view the background of the people.

CONDITIONS PRECEDING THE REVIVAL

1. *The period immediately before Hezekiah was a time of religious idolatry* (II Chron. 28:1-4). For sixteen years Ahaz poisoned the spiritual life of the people. He had "made also molten images of Baalim" (vs. 2). He forsook the temple and "burnt incense in the valley of the son of Hinnom" (vs. 3). He mixed, therefore, the worship of Molech with Baal. He also "burnt incense on the hills, and under every green tree." He even "burnt his children in the fire" (vs. 3). Human victims were offered to Baal, the sungod, to appease his anger. This was often done in droughts or depressions. Baal was the god of productivity. This productivity applied to the crops, fruits, animals, and people. When prosperity was withheld, the worshipers of Baal would often offer a human victim to assuage his wrath and

110

so they would try to bring about a return of prosperity. The prevailing religious and political condition is described in verse 19, "for he made Judah naked." This word "naked" means to cast aside all restraints. They had plummeted the depths of licentiousness. When Baal worship became the state religion, the morals decayed. It was a sensual worship. Worship reaches the hearts of the people, and its purpose is reflected in their lives. "He (Ahaz) did not that which was right" (vs. 1). There was no reason for such an abrupt departure from good. Jotham before him was a good king, and the kingdom prospered under him. Ahaz had inherited an excellent opportunity in a nation which was prosperous, but with his lapse into idolatry came religious decay, and poverty followed. In worshiping Baal he followed the example of the tribes of the Northern Kingdom.

Isaiah helps us to see their plight for he prophesied in this particular time, saying, "Come now, and let us reason together, saith the LORD: though your sins be as scarlet, they shall be as white as snow" (Isa. 1:18). Their sins are described in Isaiah's language as deep-dyed. He accuses — "from the sole of the foot even unto the head there is no soundness in it" (Isa. 1:6). Again he explains: "For Jerusalem is ruined, and Judah is fallen: because their tongue and their doings are against the LORD" (Isa. 3:8).

Hosea was preaching to Israel as well as Judah when he exclaimed, "O Israel, return unto the LORD thy God; for thou hast fallen by thine iniquity" (Hos. 14:1). All through the Book of Hosea the prophet describes the abnormal and putrid relations which earmarked God's people in this idolatrous period.

2. *It was a period of military weakness.* The Syrians smote the kingdom and carried away a multitude into captivity (II Chron. 28:5). Pekah, the ruler of the Northern Kingdom, defeated Ahaz with a great slaughter. Judah lost one hundred and twenty thousand men in the battle with Israel. Two hundred thousand of the women, sons, and daughters of Judah were carried away captive (vs. 8).

This is a moral universe. If the laws of this universe are

broken, its skies will inevitably fall in on the transgressors. During the last awful world war, many people on every hand asked the question, "Where is God? If there is a God, why doesn't He stop this awful carnage of war?" The simple answer was that it was not God's war. He did not cause the war. If the nations of the world had gotten by with the way they ignored God, and if the skies of the universe had not fallen in on our world for its transgressions, it would be proof that this is not a moral universe and that there is no God. The war did not disprove God; it rather pointed up His reality. We do not mean that the universe is operated merely by immutable law. God is over all. He executes justice and judgment. Ahaz had turned from Jehovah to many other gods. In turn he had lost two wars and hundreds of thousands of people had been slain and taken captive. This was a great price to pay for so little. Satan always exacts more than the benefit received.

3. *Diplomatic frustration ensued.* "At that time did king Ahaz send unto the kings of Assyria to help him" (vs. 16). The Edomites and Philistines were invading the cities of Judah and carrying away spoil and slaves. Ahaz had no confidence in God. It was always a sign of faithlessness when the kings formed foreign alliances. They always suffered loss by it for an alliance was a sure sign of diplomatic frustration. Two wrongs do not make a right. Ahaz was wrong to turn away from God. He was wrong again to turn to Assyria for military help. Tilgath-pilneser helped him not, but robbed him. Ahaz took sacred possessions out of the house of the Lord and valuable property from the house of the king and from the civil rulers and gave them to the king of Assyria, but it availed him nothing.

He offered sacrifices unto the gods of Syria thinking that they might help him, but "they were the ruin of him" (vs. 23). He "shut up the doors of the house of the LORD" (vs. 24). This was tantamount to breaking off all relations with Jehovah. If he did this to appease the false gods to which he had turned, he might have gone to the trouble to review history a bit and learn the results of such action. He compromised his position before God at the beginning of his reign by including Baal worship and the worship of Molech along with Jehovah worship. This act ruled out every protection and blessing of Jehovah. The false gods had never brought prosperity and national security to any ruler of Israel or Judah. Ahaz was no exception. God had signally blessed Jotham before him, for Jotham was dedicated to Jehovah. But Ahaz was too blind to detect this reality. Due to such blindness, he stumbled for sixteen years from one frustration to another. The nation needed a man of courage and vision. The nation needed a man dedicated to spiritual revival. That man was found in the king who succeeded Ahaz.

THE REVIVALIST

The revivalist was a young king. He was not one of the prophets. Three of the greatest prophets who ever lived were contemporary with Hezekiah in Judah. God often moves in strange ways. God saw fit to ordain Hezekiah, a young layman, twenty-five years old, to kindle the fires of revival. This is possibly one reason the revival began and progressed in an unorthodox style. It was no doubt greatly enhanced by great preaching, but it was not built around great preaching, nor theology. The kind of revival that Judah needed most at that time could best come through the labors of a king-evangelist, and God ordained to work through Hezekiah.

1. *Hezekiah was a man of purpose.* One expression in Hezekiah's first message to the priests and Levites revealed the purpose of his heart. "It is in mine heart to make a covenant with the LORD God of Israel" (II Chron. 29:10). He did not say it with his lips until he purposed it in his heart. Many leaders have spoken just as nobly with their lips, but what they said came to naught because it did not come from the heart. Hezekiah had bent his will before the will of God. The one obsession of the young king was to make a covenant with Jehovah. This possibly meant to renew the ancient covenant which had been brushed aside. He might have resolutely determined to re-establish the honor and

standing of his nation. He might have resolved to regain the
lost prestige of the nation and build a strong economy, but
he purposed first of all to make a covenant with God. The
wise young king believed that everything else was secondary
to spiritual religion. He purposed to promote revival. It was
his full intention to give himself completely to God and
lead his nation to do likewise. He was certain that the fierce
anger of God would not otherwise turn away from Judah.

2. *He was a man of action.* "He in the first year of his
reign, in the first month, opened the doors of the house of
the LORD" (vs. 3). He had observed the folly of Ahaz his
father. He was gravely concerned when Ahaz closed the
doors of the Lord's house, but he was helpless at that time
to do anything about it. He patiently waited for his chance.
When his father died, he immediately reopened the doors
of the Lord's house. When the doors of the Lord's house
were opened, the first signs of revival were seen. The revival spread with rapidity. Within less than two months
from the inauguration of Hezekiah, the revival had spread
to all parts of Judah and parts of the tottering Northern
Kingdom (31:1). The people generally follow their national
leaders. The people would more swiftly follow their governmental leaders in religious matters than anyone else. This
is due to the great influence they have with the people. The
revival led by Hezekiah or any other national leader is no
more short lived than a revival instigated by anyone else.
Revival never lasts much beyond one generation. The people
followed Hezekiah as readily back to God as they had
followed Jeroboam or Ahaz away from God. This places a
great responsibility for the religious destiny of a people on
those who rule the nations.

3. *The young king was a man of wisdom.* Unlike
Rehoboam he counseled with the leaders. Before instigating
the awakening he called together the religious leaders and
talked to them (29:4-11). When he felt that the revival
could best be promoted by observing the passover, he counseled with his princes and all the congregation of Judah
(30:2). He knew the value of a great assembly of all Judah

and Israel. He alone seemed to realize the spiritual impact of such a gathering. He did not force the meeting upon the leaders, however. He discussed the need and spiritual implications as well as the scriptural provisions for such a meeting. The majority decided with the king to call the assembly. Wisdom begets understanding. It is wisdom to seek counsel, and out of counsel comes wisdom.

4. *Hezekiah was a man of integrity and zeal.* "He did that which was right in the sight of the LORD, according to all that David his father had done" (29:2). The accounts in Kings and Chronicles record that several of Hezekiah's predecessors had "done that which was right in the sight of the LORD," but not as David had done. They had not demonstrated the zeal of David. Hezekiah was as devoted to Jehovah and His law as David had been. He was more zealous than the most dedicated men in his kingdom. Micah, Isaiah, and Hosea were dedicated men, but nowhere in the record do we find them calling an assembly of religious leaders and promoting a revival or putting forth a concerted effort to stamp out the worship of Baal. They cried out against the perversions and moaned the scarlet practices of their fellow citizens but they did not organize a movement back to God. It was probably providential that their preaching should prepare the way for the actions of Hezekiah.

METHODS USED IN THE REVIVAL

This great revival is best seen and understood in the light of the methods employed to produce it. The task that lay before Hezekiah was difficult, and for many great men it would have been impossible. He began by opening and repairing the doors of the temple (29:3). The closed doors had been a symbol of national repudiation of Jehovah worship. The first step in the right direction was to open them. Judah could not be reconciled to God as long as the temple doors were closed. Through the open doors Judah would have access to God.

Judah was in a bad condition economically and had lost her place politically among the nations. The king did

not begin with either of these urgent needs. He began with
the spiritual need. He put first things first. There are three
steps in the death of a nation. First, it turns from God and
dies spiritually. Second, its economy withers. The fact that
the economy of a nation dries up when the nation loses its
religious stamina is a matter of history. Third, when the
economy dries up and there is not enough food and shelter
for the people, they become a discontented and easy prey
to designing forces from within and pressure groups from
without. No nation will die as long as it is spiritually strong.
Hezekiah began at the correct place — he began with God.[1]

1. *He gathered the priests and Levites to give them
instructions* (vs. 5). He called for them. They did not insti-
gate the restoral of temple worship. If they had done their
part all along, it might have been different with the nation.
They had become cold and professional. Being cold, professional, and spiritually blind, it took a consecrated person
from without to awaken them. The young king made a very
impressive and enlightening speech before the priests and
Levites.

(1)   He confessed the sins of their fathers as well
as their own sins (vs. 6). He did not say, "The sins of my
father," but he said, "For our fathers have trespassed." The
priest Urijah had joined Ahaz in setting up idolatrous worship. They had turned their backs upon God. When people
turn their faces from the house of God and from the worship
of Jehovah, they turn themselves away from God. Many
think themselves to be good Christians and within the will
of God because they read their Bibles and pray, but they
never frequent the house of God. Such example is dangerous. When one chooses a principle for his life, he should ask
the question, "What would happen if everyone else should
adopt this same principle?" If everyone who claims to worship God is not an integral part of a congregation and does
not attend the Lord's house, it would be but a short time
until there would be no holy assembly. There would be no
church to preach the Gospel of Christ, and the whole world
would be in darkness.

(2) *Hezekiah pointed up certain blunders which had been made* (vs. 7). They had not only shut up the doors of the Lord's house, but they had put out the lamps and had not burned incense nor offered burnt offerings in the holy place. The lamps signified the light of God and were a symbol of the open Word of God. Where the Word of God is not read and expounded, there is no spiritual light and the path of the people becomes darkened and obscure. This caused the people to stumble. They had not "burned incense." This, to the Hebrews, denoted prayer and praise. They had forsaken the altar of prayer. They had been so preoccupied with material things and so darkened by the evils around them that they had not praised God.

(3) He called their attention to the consequences of such neglect (vss. 8-9). Such blunders had invoked the wrath of God. They were in "trouble." This word "trouble" indicates that they were being tossed about as a ship tossed upon the waves of a storm-swept sea. They had become the object of ridicule and hissing from the peoples without. The young king was endeavoring to cause the religious leaders to inquire of themselves as to why these things happened. Up to now they had doubtlessly felt no guilt for the national decay which was evident all around them. Disaster and calamity is not always the sign that someone has sinned or erred in high place of leadership. But many times it is. The king was bringing these religious leaders face to face with the consequences of sin and their share in this calamity.

(4) The young king inspired the religious leaders. "My sons, be not now negligent: for the Lord hath chosen you to stand before him, to serve him, and that ye should minister unto him, and burn incense" (vs. 11). It is significant to notice that in verse 5 he called them "ye Levites," to remind them of their obligation to God as religious leaders. In verse 11 he called them "my sons," to remind them of their relation to him. The relationship was that of a father and his sons. He would expect cooperation of his sons. They were to serve with him in bringing revival

to the land. He was direct and tender and got results. This particular speech before these religious leaders had much to do with what followed in the weeks ahead.

He said, "be not now negligent." He was urging them to steer away from carelessness which might retard the work. He had told them what to do. He had urged upon them to cleanse themselves and to cleanse the temple. Now he was inspiring them to do it. There is as much value in inspiration as there is in instruction. Magnificent and well-phrased instructions will not necessarily move a people to action. It is necessary to give them certain instruction, but it is just as necessary to inspire them to perform the task. "For the LORD hath chosen you to stand before him" (vs. 11). They were to stand before God first and the congregation second. They were to please God and not the congregation. It was a signal honor to be chosen of God to stand before Him. It carried with it a corresponding responsibility.

2.   *Hezekiah arranged a great opening worship service* (vss. 20-36). "Went up to the house of the LORD" (vs. 20). The king restored temple worship. Several significant things took place at this great opening service. They observed the sin offering, burnt offering, and thank offering.

(1)   The sin offering (vs. 21). This was the most important aspect of the ritual observed by Hezekiah. They made "a sin offering for the kingdom, and for the sanctuary, and for Judah." "For the kingdom" meant the kingly house.[2] Ahaz had broken the covenant and led the people into great sin, and Hezekiah was making a sin offering for the ruling house to atone for the breach. "For the sanctuary" refers to the personnel of the temple; i.e., the priest and Levites. It was necessary to include them in this part of the worship. "And for Judah" means all the people. They had all corrupted themselves. They felt that an atonement must be made. It was not enough to lament and forsake their sins, but they must atone for their sins. They brought therefore a sin offering.

According to Leviticus 4:13-21, when the congregation

made a sin offering, it was to consist of *one* young bullock. This practice is borne out in Numbers 15:24. But here seven rams, seven lambs, and seven goats are offered because this was an extraordinary occasion. The sins were great and of long duration. When the bullocks were killed, the priests received "the blood, and sprinkled it on the altar" (vs. 22). And in like manner they did with the blood of the rams and of the lambs. Dr. Wilbur M. Smith points up that this was the first time in over eight hundred years, with one exception which was insincere and unscriptural, that "blood" is referred to as part of the sacrifice offered by the Israelites.[3] Blood is mentioned in the records during these years but not in connection with sacrifice. The blood here was not sprinkled upon the altar with the finger as required in the law (Lev. 4:17), but it was dashed against the altar.[4] "They laid their hands upon" the goats. The representatives performed this service and not the people (Lev. 4:15). By this symbol they wish their sins to be transferred to the sacrifice. They thereby were reconciled to God. The goat became the sin offering. "For he hath made him to be sin for us, who knew no sin; that we might be made the righteousness of God in him" (II Cor. 5:21). Christ was made our sin offering in the same manner as is represented here.

(2) The burnt offering (vs. 24). This was the second stage in their return to God.[5] The offering was consumed by fire. Fire signified purification. The burnt offering was an expression of their consecration to Jehovah. Their forgiven selves were laid on the altar of undivided devotion to God. While the offering was being consumed by fire, it was natural for them to hear the joyful sound of music and to join in songs of praise to God. "And the Levites stood with the instruments of David, and the priests with the trumpets" (vs. 26). When the burnt offering began, the people began to sing the songs of Jehovah (vs. 27). They continued playing instruments and singing until the offering ceased. When the offering ceased, the king and all the people "bowed themselves, and worshiped" (vs. 29). This

means that at first they bowed down on their knees, then they prostrated themselves completely before the Lord. It is not enough to attend worship services and be where God is worshiped, but all must wholeheartedly participate in worship.

(3) The thank offering. The people themselves suggested the third great step in their return to God. "Then Hezekiah answered" (vs. 31). This expression signifies that the people had suggested it. The thank offering is a life of service. They dedicated themselves in the burnt offering, but it was necessary to further involve all their achievements of the future. All one is now and ever hopes to be, he brings to God. It consists of the fruits of one's labors. It consists of the ties, the honors, and the glory which one may receive in the future. It was necessary to bring a sacrifice of alms, as well as praise to God. The offering was immense. Out of hearts of gratitude the liberal offering surprised the king as well as the entire congregation (vss. 32-36). Liberality is one of the earmarks of revival. People cannot worship God and mammon at the same time. When revival comes, repentant people worship only God. They are less attached to property, and their hearts are liberal. The offering was so generously given and was in such quantity that it became evident it was a spiritual movement and not an ecclesiastical reformation initiated by the ruling authorities.[6]

3. *Israel and Judah united to observe the Passover at Jerusalem.* The passover was instituted as a memorial to the delivery of the children of Israel from the Egyptian bondage. The time of observance began the fourteenth day of the first month, which was April (Num. 9:1-3). Hezekiah had counseled with the princes and all the congregation of Judah and had decided to observe it the second month (II Chron. 30:2). They were afraid that if they should wait an entire year to observe this great religious festival, the religious fervor of the people would cool and it would not be as effective. His suggestion may have been opposed by many who would prefer deferring it at all risks. There are

always those who prefer the letter to the spirit. Hezekiah was not entirely outside the law in his proposed observance in the second month. The law actually permitted such a postponement (Num. 9:10-11). It was allowable to observe it the fourteenth day of the second month if the reason was valid. The reason offered by Hezekiah was valid, for the people were unclean and were not ready to participate in the observance of the Passover at the proper time.

"All Israel" was invited. The writer of Chronicles takes no note of the political condition of Israel. But Israel was so politically weak at this time that Hezekiah could venture to do what earlier kings of Judah would have feared to do.

(1) A proclamation was made (30:5) that throughout all the land the people should come to Jerusalem to keep the Passover. The statement, "of a long time in such sort as it was written," refers to Israel and not Judah. This was the first attempt to draw Israel en masse to the Passover.

(2) They sent letters to all Israel and Judah (vs. 6). The letter contained several appeals.

(a) It was a call to "turn again unto the LORD God of Abraham" (vs. 6). It was an appeal to desist from rebellion "and be not like your fathers . . . which trespassed against the LORD God who . . . gave them up to desolation" (vs. 7). God had given them up to be an astonishment. They had astonished the world with their spiritual blindness and moral degradation. This was no reputation of which they could be proud.

(b) "Yield yourselves unto the LORD (vs. 8). It literally means, "give the hand." Consent to take Him for your God. It referred to a handshake, sealing a bargain which had been made. They were urged to enter into an agreement with God and seal it with a handclasp.

(c) They were urged "to enter into his sanctuary . . . and serve the LORD your God, that the fierceness of his wrath may turn away from you" (vs. 8).

(d)   The letters reminded the people of the graciousness and mercy of God. God's face would be with them once again if they would return unto Him.

(3)   The response to the letters was mixed. In Israel some mocked. Some "laughed them to scorn, and mocked them" (vs. 10). The surviving towns and villages as a whole throughout Israel mocked, and Hezekiah's appeal failed. But some individuals responded to his letter more favorably. Multitudes of individuals "of Asher and Manasseh and of Zebulun humbled themselves, and came to Jerusalem" (vs. 11). The language of this text indicates why other multitudes did not come to Jerusalem. It was pride. They no doubt had the heart hunger, but their pride was too much for a letter to break down. The fact that some humbled themselves shows why many refused. There was wholehearted acceptance in Judah (vs. 12).

(4)   "A very great congregation" (vs. 13) assembled in Jerusalem for the Passover. Multitudes from the Northern Kingdom and an overwhelming number from Judah came to Jerusalem. This is the first written reference to the Passover for over seven hundred years in the history of the Hebrew people.[7] We know the Passover had been celebrated during these years but there is no record to that end. The revival for the whole nation depended upon the truth symbolized by the Passover. Long before God had delivered Israel from Egyptian bondage, and He must now again break the chains of pagan philosophies and heathen worship and set them free.

The lamb was killed, and the priests sprinkled the blood on the altar (vss. 15-16). Without the blood there could have been no revival. The lamb was a symbol of the Lamb whose blood would atone for the sins of the whole world. "As long as there is an ignorance of the Cross, or a perverted conception of the meaning of the Cross, or an abhorrence of the precious blood of the Son of God . . . a revival cannot come, at least a revival that saves the souls of men."[8]

Some irregularities prevailed (vss. 17-18). The rites
were performed with difficulty because neither the priests
nor Levites were familiar with the rites of the festival. The
nation had been blinded so long by idolatry and the feast
had been so long neglected that many of the worshipers
were unclean. They had not properly cleansed themselves
for the festival, and they partook "otherwise than it was
written" (vs. 18). They were ignorant of the requirements
of the ceremony. It is likely that Hezekiah knew this when
he invited them to come to Jerusalem and participate. This
was particularly true of the people from the Northern
Empire. It would have been unwise and disastrous to
dampen their new zeal by excluding them from the festival
because they did not meet the letter of the law. Multitudes
of them were from the Northern tribes who had "humbled
themselves" and accepted Hezekiah's invitation, while the
majority of their brethren scornfully rejected it. They were
allowed to take part in the Passover irrespective of their
uncleanness. The law said that the penalty was death for
anyone who attended the festival in a state of unprepared-
ness (Lev. 15:31). If divine punishment fell on them, it
would also defeat the purpose of the assembly. Panic instead
of revival would be the result. Great distress rather than
sweet fellowship would characterize the meeting. Neither
the priest nor one of the prophets but the young king-re-
vivalist himself came forward to meet the serious situation
produced by these irregularities. "But Hezekiah prayed for
them" (vs. 18). Jehovah heard him and "healed the people"
(vs. 20). Either a pestilence had already begun or fear of an
outbreak of disease had seized the people. God either healed
them from actual disease or removed the fear of such. God
is a merciful God. He is willing to exercise grace and to hear
a repentant people. Prayer always prevails. Just as Samuel
had prayed for his people at Mizpeh, so it became necessary that Hezekiah pray in Jerusalem for his people. In both
instances prayer made the difference between defeat and
victory: between tragedy and revival.

"Great gladness" characterized the fourteen days of festival (vs. 21). During these two weeks the king, governmental officials, priests, Levites, Jews, and Israelites rejoiced in the Lord. They praised Jehovah with singing and loud instruments. Just as gladness characterized the opening service a month before (29:30), so once again the great multitude from all over the land rejoiced.

People were given vital instructions (30:22). The Scriptures were opened and read, and the people were taught things about God and their duty to Him. This was necessary because they had been without the Word of God for years. Their souls were starved. Hezekiah spoke encouragingly to the Levites, and they seemed to have done the bulk of the teaching and preaching. He urged them to study diligently and feed the people the pure Word of God. A very great congregation had gathered, and such an opportunity to preach the Word of God might not come again in a long time. This teaching and preaching of the Word undoubtedly played a tremendous role in the revival.

At this point it might be well to point out that this was not the only teaching and preaching which had been done in the land. As we have already noticed, Isaiah, Hosea, and Micah were preaching in Judah. We must not forget that contemporaneously Amos was preaching to the remnants of the northern tribes. It is very likely that the fervent preaching of Amos in the north had been responsible for multitudes of the northern Israelites accepting the cordial invitation of Hezekiah to come to Jerusalem for this festival. It is likely that the reason for the great place the Word of God was given in this revival is seen in the preaching of Isaiah, Hosea, and Micah.

The mighty, earnest preaching of Isaiah must have been of great effect in preparation for this revival though nothing is said in his book about it. He preached fearlessly the very ideas which were used to lay the foundation for the revival. The preaching of Isaiah was a factor in the popular response given the revival methods of Hezekiah. Isaiah moved with

poise among the ruling families of Judah and hurled demol-
ishing missiles into their hearts. He was polished and dynamic. His messages were pointed and effective. He was en-
couraging in his applications. God gave him clear messianic
conceptions. Messianic revelation reached its highest level
in the preaching of Isaiah at this very time.

Hosea prophesied contemporaneously with Hezekiah.
His preaching was direct. The direct preaching of Hosea,
added to the voice of Isaiah, must have probed the conscience of the people. Conscience is the greatest ally of the
revivalist. Hezekiah's emphasis on ritual would not have
received a ready response had not the conscience of the
people been awakened by Hosea. The Book of Hosea
describes the people of God in Israel and Judah in two
expressions: "Lo-ammi" (Hos. 1:9), which means "not my
people," and "Ammi" (Hos. 2:1), which means "my people."
Under Ahaz Judah had alienated itself from Jehovah by
apostasy. Hosea was gifted with illustrations. He used the
illustration of the unfaithful wife to shame and prod the
people. Only the judgment will reveal the effects of the
preaching of Hosea in this particular revival period.

Micah also lived and preached in Hezekiah's day. The
expression, "to hissing," (II Chron. 29:8) used by Hezekiah
in his speech to the priests and Levites was no doubt bor-
rowed from Micah (Mic. 6:16). Micah had great influence
on Hezekiah and the people of Judah. "Micah the Morasthite
prophesied in the days of Hezekiah king of Judah, and spake
to all the people of Judah, saying, Thus saith the LORD of
hosts; Zion shall be plowed like a field, and Jerusalem shall
become heaps, and the mountain of the house as the high
places of a forest" (Jer. 26:18). The king and the people
heeded the warning of Micah, and God repented the judgment He had determined to send upon them. Micah made
three great contributions: He pleaded earnestly with Judah;
he gave them some plain instructions; and he gave them
future hope. He told them that one day the Messiah would
come from "Bethlehem Ephratah . . . of Judah" (Mic. 5:2).

The people confessed their sins unto God (II Chron. 30:22). With all this backlog of preaching and with the spiritual momentum of this great gathering, they were ready in heart and mind to confess to God. The presence of God was manifest in the gathering; the Word of God was taught; and when these two phenomena are present, confession of sins follows. When a sense of God's presence prevails and the Word of God is made known, people become so conscious of sin that they are compelled to do something about it. It is worthwhile to notice that they confessed to God and not to the priest. "Making confession to the LORD God of their fathers" (vs. 22). Revival under this circumstance was inevitable.

ACCOMPLISHMENTS OF THE REVIVAL

1. *The idols were destroyed* (II Chron. 31:1). When these people who had assembled at Jerusalem went back to their respective towns and villages, they destroyed the images of Baal and other gods. This image destruction took place in the communities of the northern tribes as well as in Judah. This action was the natural fruit of repentance. They had heard the Word of God, and they had felt the presence of God. Their eyes had been opened, the scales of blindness had fallen off, and their minds about God had been changed. They had experienced a change of heart. The idols had to go. They could no longer countenance those ugly vitiations of Jehovah.

2. *The revival brought a return to public worship.* The doors of the temple had been closed before the revival. The revival began when the king opened the doors of worship. Large crowds attended worship during the revival. The Passover held at Jerusalem was the largest religious gathering since Solomon. The very first assembly of worship called by Hezekiah brought an overwhelming attendance. The thank offerings were so large and the burnt offerings so many that they did not have enough priests to perform the ceremonies (29:34). The Levites were called upon to assist in the emergency.

3. *The people practiced holy living.* The priests and Levites had accepted Hezekiah's challenge to sanctify themselves (30:15). The people were taught the value of cleanliness (vss. 17-20). "A constant recurrence of such words as *cleanse, consecrate, purification, holiness, the Holy Place, holy things,* and especially, the verb *sanctify,* which occurs fourteen times,"[9] indicates a return to holy living. Revival always changes the lives of the individuals. It changes the tone of a nation and the activities of whole communities. This was seen in the Frontier Revival in 1800 in America. Men who were drunkards, murderers, and without principle before the revival were completely changed in the course of the revival. It was even unsafe to travel on the frontier until the revival began in Logan County, Kentucky, and spread all across the West. By 1801 there was a marked change. Noisy and explosive communities had become peaceable and safe. It was as if the atmosphere of heaven had settled upon the once feverish and sinful areas and transformed them into colonies of righteousness.

4. *The revival was characterized by a return of prosperity.* "And Hezekiah had exceeding much riches and honour" (32:27). The nation was blessed financially. They had an abundance of silver, gold, and precious stones. This stands in marked contrast to the financial destitution under Ahaz who reigned before the revival. The people had been impoverished under Ahaz' reign because of military defeats (28:17-21) and draining alliances (28:16). They had become so weak militarily and financially that Ahaz was desperate. He became so desperate that he offered sacrifices to the gods of Syria, hoping that they would help him in his weakness (28:23). After the revival Hezekiah had so much gold and silver that many things were fashioned out of these precious metals. All the wealth and honor continued to multiply in spite of Sennacherib's effort to invade and destroy Hezekiah and his people.

The crops were bountiful and animals multiplied (32:28). New barns were erected to house the bounteous increase in corn, and stalls were multiplied to house the fat cattle. God blessed Hezekiah with much substance. Walls were erected to protect the rich possessions from robbers. Spiritual upsurge is always accompanied with a period of prosperity. The nation should never resort to faulty principles to prime the pump of economy. Ahaz tried every means to bolster his declining economy. Hezekiah turned only to God and built his economy around time-tried measures of righteousness. It brought spiritual revival and revival gives rise to healthy economy.

CHAPTER 8

THE REVIVAL UNDER JOSIAH

II Chronicles 34:1-33; 35:1-19

The devotion of a good king, coupled with the rediscovery of the books of the law, formed the background of
the revival in Judah in the last years of the seventh century
before Christ. The nation had gradually drifted away from
God. For almost a hundred years there had been no revival.
The last two kings were wicked rulers. Temple worship was
unknown, and the Holy Place was in a bad state of repairs.
The book of the law was lost and religious abominations
filled the land. The priests of Judah were defiled, and murder and intrigue reeked in the king's court. A youth, eight
years old, came to the throne of Judah. He became known
as "good King Josiah." The traits of character and destiny
which determine the course of men's lives almost always
manifest themselves early. This was true of Josiah.

THE CONVERSION OF JOSIAH THE KING

For fifty-seven years alien faiths had been entrenching
themselves in the land. The two previous reigns had let the
nation disintegrate spiritually. Manasseh had ruled for fifty-
five years. During his reign the "high places" had been
restored, and he copied "like unto the abominations of the
heathen" (II Chron. 33:2). His folly weakened the people.
The kingdom was overrun by the Assyrians, and Manasseh
was carried away into captivity. In captivity he humbled
himself before God and prayed unto God. God heard his
confession of repentance. He was brought again unto Jeru-

salem and then "Manasseh knew that the LORD he was God"
(33:13). On his return to Jerusalem to reign, he performed a
weak reformation, but he did not live long enough to make
up for the evil seeds he had sown in his earlier reign. At the
death of Manasseh, Amon his son, came to the throne. Amon
did wickedly after the example of his father. After two years
he was assassinated by his servants in the palace. The
people had had their fill of plots and political intrigue.
They slew all those who murdered Amon. They cleared out
the political filth of the court. This action of the people was
a healthy sign. It was the nearest thing to democracy found
anywhere in the history of the nation.[1]

Josiah began to reign about 642 B.C. at the age of
eight. When he was sixteen years old, "he began to seek
after the God of David his father" (34:3). His conversion
could have been the result of many things. He was no doubt
disgusted with the extreme evil policies of his father and
grandfather. He had possibly read from the records the
experiences of his grandfather, Manasseh. He had either
been told by some of the court attendants, or he had read
how his grandfather turned from his evil ways in his last
days. This may have had some bearing on his conversion.
Those who taught him did not have access to the book of
the law and taught him what others from memory had
taught them.[2] He was also influenced by Huldah, the
prophetess who respected him (34:26-28), and by Jeremiah
who praised him. Jeremiah referred to the good King Josiah
when he wrote, "He judged the cause of the poor and
needy; then it was well with him: was not this to know me?
saith the LORD" (Jer. 22:16). Disgusted with his father,
moved by the record of the last days of his grandfather,
and influenced by the religious teachers in his court and the
preaching of Jeremiah, he was led to seek the Lord. He was
converted. A tree is known by the fruit it bears. He immediately began a period of reformation.

HIS REFORMATION

The reformation under Josiah was twofold: "He began to purge Judah and Jerusalem from the high places, and the groves, and the carved images, and the molten images" (34:3); and he began a drive to raise money to repair the temple.

1. *Josiah personally supervised the destruction of the idols* (II Chron. 34:7). For six years he prosecuted his iconoclastic policy.[3] The accounts of the reformation given in II Chronicles and II Kings supplement each other. The account in II Kings does not claim that the reformation took place after the discovery of the book of the law and thus it is not dated. But the account in II Chronicles is dated, and it claims that the major part of the reformation took place before the discovery of the law.

Josiah did two things in the reformation which revealed a trait of ferocity. He broke down the molten images, beat them into pieces, and "made dust of them, and strowed it upon the graves of them that had sacrificed unto them" (vs. 4). In strowing the dust of the images upon the graves, he virtually proclaimed the helplessness of both the false gods which had been worshiped and the dead worshipers.[4] Josiah also burned the bones of the priests upon the altar of Bethel and polluted it as the prophet years before had declared it (II Kings 23:16). This particular incident indicates that the reformation was not confined to Judah alone but included parts of Israel.

2. *He repaired the temple.* Josiah waited six years from the time he began the reformation until he actually undertook to repair the temple. The work on the temple might have been deliberately delayed because of a strong feeling which had arisen among the people when the idols and altars to the false gods were destroyed. The weight of opinion, however, would declare that the reason for the delay was lack of funds with which to begin and complete the work. It would have required considerable time to raise enough money to repair the temple. The temple had not been in use by the people for at least seventy-five years. Ne-

glect was not the main reason for the needed repair. When the Assyrians had besieged the city of Jerusalem and carried away Manasseh as captive, the temple was very likely badly damaged.

Josiah personally supervised the extirpation of the idols, but he was wise enough to relegate responsibility in repairing the temple. He chose laymen to direct this work. The work of Joash had been impeded by priests who were proficient in collecting money for the temple, but dilatory in using it to repair the temple (II Kings 12:8). Josiah profited from the mistake of Joash, and he chose three outstanding laymen to supervise the work. He selected Shaphan the scribe, Maaseiah the mayor of the city, and Joah the historian.

The work was done faithfully (II Chron. 34:12). The contractors, foreman, and musicians, all alike did their work well. The three laymen who were over all worked out a thorough organization and placed definite responsibility on the builders. They were more than well organized, for they worked with a song in their hearts. "And other of the Levites, all that could skill of instruments of musick" (vs. 12). When hearts are filled with music, men can build for God; but without it, they labor under the foreman of duty rather than the inspiration of privilege.

THE BOOK OF THE LAW DISCOVERED

In the process of repairing the temple, the book of the law was found (vs. 14). When they removed the collection of money gathered to repair the temple, Hilkiah the high priest found the scroll. If Josiah had not been busy doing good and repairing the temple, the book of the law would not have been found. The rediscovery of the law was a greater achievement than the repairing of the temple. Many blessings lie ahead for the faithful. The faithful child of God will often accomplish more as he moves toward his goal than will be done in achieving the goal itself. Some think the book was found under a pile of stones in the temple where it was hidden when Ahaz burned the other copies of the law.[5] Geikie says that Thenius, a thorough and impartial scholar of his day, claimed that it was hidden in the ark of the covenant which Manasseh had thrown into one of the chambers of the temple where it remained unnoticed for years.[6] Since the temple had been closed for seventy-five years to the use of the people, this view is quite plausible. The finding of the book of the law marked the beginning of the revival. The book found by Hilkiah was believed by the writer of II Chronicles to be the whole Pentateuch, and that Shaphan did not read all the book to the king but only read "therein" as indicated by verse 18.[7] Many scholars believe it was only the Book of Deuteronomy. This view was held by DeWitt, Reuss, Schrader, Ewall, Jerome, Pracopius of Gaza, and Chrysostom. Geikie says that it is reasonable to hold that Hilkiah found Deuteronomy and various other sacred writings which were at that time comprised in the law.[8] The portion read by Shaphan to the king was the Book of Deuteronomy before its final revision.[9] It would have required about three hours to read the entire Book of Deuteronomy. To read the entire Pentateuch would have required no less than ten hours. It is very probable that only the Book of Deuteronomy was read in full to the king.

It does not really matter for our study here how much of the law was rediscovered by Hilkiah, but the writer goes along with the ancient chronicler that it comprised the entire Pentateuch. Ewall in *Geschichte*, Vol. 3, p. 759, reminds us that a book containing more or less of the Pentateuch as we have it now was in circulation long before Josiah.[10] The book of the law found by Hilkiah was written by Moses and not by Jeremiah or any of his contemporaries or some post-exilic author. Deuteronomy claims Moses as the writer. "And it came to pass, when Moses had made an end of writing the words of this law in a book, until they were finished, that Moses commanded the Levites, which bare the ark of covenant of the LORD, saying, Take this book of the law, and put it in the side of the ark . . ." (Deut.

31:24-26). Keil believes that Moses wrote at least the first thirty-one chapters of Deuteronomy.[11]

The fact that the book was found is another evidence of the indestructibleness of the Word of God.[12] Despite the fact that God's people were fickle, that the priests and rulers were often godless, and that many other perils threatened the destruction of the written Word of God, it did not perish. It survived the indifference of its friends, the ravages of time, and the wilful plans of Satan. The reverberation of heavy voices and the lightning-like brilliance of sharp penknives of many weighty critics besiege the Bible in our day. One would almost be afraid for the Book if he should forget the perils through which the Word has come through the centuries. The Bible will survive, of this we have no doubt. But will the generation which loses knowledge of it? This is our concern.

1. *The scroll was read to the king* (vs. 18). Hilkiah gave the scroll to Shaphan the scribe, who read it to Josiah. The content of the book was news to the king. At first it was sad news. "He rent his clothes" (vs. 19) indicates sadness and repentance. The news was frightening. He had done the best he knew. But according to the law, he was wrong about some things, and his goodness had fallen short. When he heard from the law what Jehovah would do to his people if they compromised the truth, he was deeply moved. When he saw how wrong he and the people had been about many things, he was humbled.[13] He was repentant rather than resentful. He was unlike Asa in this respect. Like Asa he had accomplished a great work, but when he realized his mistakes, he bent his will before the truth. Things which he had tolerated appeared to be intolerable in the light of the law. He was convinced that he must walk by the Word of God.

The king sent several of his most trusted men to inquire of the Lord for him and for the people. He sent them to see if there was any way to avert the judgments of the Lord which were due to fall upon them. It appears here that the inquiry was to be twofold; they were to pray unto God, and to counsel with the prophetess, Huldah. True repentance brings sorrow for abuses, but it also creates a desire to know how things may be rectified. The law and the gospel operate in conjunction with each other. The law reveals one's need, and the gospel provides the answer to the need. This answer becomes good news. They went to Huldah the prophetess. This title is given also to Miriam (Exod. 15:20), Deborah (Judg. 4:4), Anna (Luke 2:36), and Noadiah (Neh. 6:14). This incidentally implies the lofty position which good women held in the religious society fashioned by Jehovah.

Huldah's reply contained two parts. She warned the king that all the judgments referred to in the law would come upon the people because they had forsaken God. The sins of the repentant people would be forgiven, but they must suffer the consequences. Huldah's prophecy that Judah was doomed to destruction was in keeping with the message of Jeremiah that nothing could prevent the fall of Judah. She assured the king that the judgments would not come in his day. She attributed the delay of the judgments to his humility and tenderness of heart (II Chron. 34:27). Revival finds roots in a tender heart. The post-captivity revival began in the tender heart of Nehemiah. The revival under Josiah began in his tender heart and spread to all the people.

2. *The book was read to the people and their leaders* (vs. 30). The book told its own story. There was no exposition of the law as was given later by Ezra and the Levites who assisted him in the post-captivity revival. The entire book was read to them at one hearing. Josiah read the book to his people "and he read in their ears all the words of the book" (vs. 30). By this means the people heard God speak. It startled them. It smote them with the realization that they had ignored and offended God. They realized that they were as guilty as if their sins had been wilfully committed. Fear prevailed, and they stood bareheaded before God. This is the sign of the beginning of real revival. They saw and heard God in the words of the law. It was the vision of God

which stirred them. They never saw their sins nor realized their guilt until they heard the law. When men look at their sins through the presence of God, they recognize the ugliness of sin. When this happens, they become disgusted with their sins and turn from them to God. The Word of God kindled revival fires among Josiah's subjects.

Men act when God speaks. When Abraham heard God speak, he left his family and native land to go into a strange place to do the will of God. When Samuel heard God speak, he said, "Speak, Lord, for thy servant heareth." It marked a new and bold venture for him. Paul heard God speak and gave up the security of rabbiship to hazard his life and destiny for a mighty cause. Francis of Assisi heard the small voice of God and denounced riches and luxury for the dreary life of a Friar. All of these and scores of others who heard and heeded the Word of God became instruments in God's hands to bring great spiritual awakenings to the world.

The Bible gives light. It provides power. It is better than authority. "Not by might, nor by power, but by my spirit, saith the Lord of hosts" (Zech. 4:6). Dr. J. B. Lawrence gives us a classic illustration of the need of divine power and light. He says that some years past he was riding on a streetcar when suddenly there was a blinding flash, and the car stopped. The fuse had blown out. While the fuse was being replaced, they sat in darkness. The car was powerless to move. In the cable above there was ample power, but because there was no contact, the streetcar was dark and still.[14] This was the case in Josiah's day. There were ample power and light available, but there was no contact. They were in spiritual darkness. They had not the Word of God. Without knowledge of it, they sat lifeless and blind.

3. *A covenant was made* (II Chron. 34:31-32). When Josiah concluded reading the law, he stood up by a pillar in plain view of the people. He made a covenant with the Lord to obey all the words of the book and urged the people to a similar pledge. God's people have always been a cove-

nant people. When they forget their solemn pledges to God, they go astray. When they renew their vows to God, they are strong. They agreed "to walk after the LORD," i.e., to worship the Lord. They further agreed to "keep his commandments," i.e., all the laws of God including the moral, civil, and ceremonial precepts. They pledged to do all these things with the whole heart. They would worship Jehovah, keeping all His commandments faithfully and with marked sincerity. They vowed to perform all the words found in the book which had been read to them. They stood to indicate the seal of their solemn oath. It is not sufficient to resolve in the heart, nor is it enough to declare a covenant with the lips. It must receive a permanent seal. When they "stood to it," that was the seal. Sinners may resolve to accept Christ and live the good life, but unless they walk out in a public declaration of their inward vow, the devil can easily steal away their good intentions.

4. *Further reforms were natural after the instructions of the law.* Josiah and the people recognized that compromise was out of the question if they were to keep the solemn covenant into which they had entered with God. All the abominations were removed. Certain practices which formally did not appear bad now stood out as sickening to God and to the sober-minded. The people were led to serve God. It involved total service. The whole life with every ambition and desire and plan was to be lived with one supreme goal and view: to serve Jehovah. They returned to a theocratic system for the individual and the nation.

5. *The Passover was observed.* When the remaining abominations of the pagans were removed, they celebrated the Passover in Jerusalem (II Chron. 35:1). This observance surpassed the great observance in Hezekiah's day. Hezekiah's Passover eclipsed all Passover convocations clear back to Solomon's time. But Josiah's Passover went back beyond Solomon to Samuel (vs. 18). It was attended by all Judah and by more from Israel than had come to Hezekiah's festival. Jewish life was enriched by the great religious festivals. Almost all great revivals in Hebrew history were connected

with the great religious convocations. The religious festivals
were holy days and not merely holidays. Western civilization suffers, because its great festivals and periods of leisure
are divorced from a religious consecration.[15] Holidays in our
nation, including Easter and Christmas, have become periods
of frivolity, drinking, and great slaughter on the highways.
They are periods of grief and regret rather than revival. We
are letting go one of our most golden religious opportunities
to reach the souls of men.

(1) The priests were placed in their office to
serve with cheerfulness and constancy. The Levites who
were responsible to teach the laity were given special instructions and sent out to prepare the nation for the
approaching Passover. They taught the folk how to worship
Jehovah and how to properly observe the Passover. When
the people were prepared, the Passover was observed on the
fourteenth day of April. The great multitude of families
which partook of the Passover were from many different
villages and cities from both Judah and Israel. They were of
various opinions. Their backgrounds were different. Some
were better prepared than others and understood the purpose of the Passover more clearly. However, it is safe to
assume that there were very few who did not benefit spiritually from the mighty convocation.

(2) Various numbers attending the feast did not
possess the paschal lamb. Due to ignorance, poverty, and
distance traveled, many of them were dependent on the
king, his princes, and the priests and Levites to provide the
paschal lamb (vss. 7-8). The Passover was observed with
great care. The priests and Levites were careful to see that
everything was done in strict compliance with the law.

(3) The influence of the celebration was felt in
many areas of life. It declared the restoration of Jehovah
worship. It revived holy enthusiasm in many to serve God.
From the experiences of this festival stemmed the loyalty of
temple worship at Jerusalem that endured until the city was
captured by Nebuchadnezzar. The Hebrews who attended
the Passover took the spirit of consecration and loyalty back

to Shechem, Shiloh, Samaria, and many other cities and villages of Judah and Israel.[16]

(4)   Jeremiah, the young prophet of Anathoth, spread revival fires throughout the land by urging his fellow prophets and religious teachers to teach the words of the newly found book of the law to the people and to warn them, "Cursed be the man that obeyeth not the words of this covenant" (Jer. 11:3). He obeyed the commission of God to make known the words of the newly-found law to all the people of the kingdom (Jer. 11:6-8). It is not known how long Jeremiah traveled from village to village and revealed the details of the book of the law, but the effects are undeniable. A mild revival of spiritual religion spread everywhere, but many refused to be affected by the wave of godliness. There was opposition to Jeremiah for his plain speaking, and groups formed conspiracy against Josiah (Jer. 11:9-13). The revival was thorough enough, however, to provide a firm basis for material development. The great Passover took place 624 B.C. in the eighteenth year of the reign of Josiah, and he lived and reigned at least twelve more years. Little is said of these years, but with the preaching and teaching of Jeremiah and the vigorous promotion of Josiah, we know these years were momentous. The resources of the nation were developed, and the nation became stronger internally. The army was reorganized and became too eager militarily. All accounts implied great progress and advancement in every area of national life.

LESSONS FOR OUR GENERATION

1. *The place of the books of the law in the revivals of the Old Testament*. To understand and appreciate the revivals of the Old Testament it is necessary to study carefully the Pentateuch and particularly Deuteronomy. Most of the Old Testament revivals were stimulated by reading and expounding the law and by a return to God's commandments and precepts. The text for the Mount Carmel revival was Deuteronomy 11:17. The revival under Hezekiah was promoted and inspired around the ritual of Leviticus and

Deuteronomy. The revival in Josiah's time came from the rediscovery of the book of the law. The post-captivity revival was born when Ezra read the law from a wooden pulpit in the streets of Jerusalem and the Levites expounded it to the entire congregation. These great revivals of the Old Testament constitute some of our most precious treasures of revival history. A fresh knowledge of the books of the law is essential to a comprehensive study of these mighty events.

2. *The tendency of men to forget God and to lapse into sin.* Adam sinned in the garden and fell from a lofty state, and this was the pattern followed through the centuries. God called Abraham and gave special favor to him and unique revelations to his descendants, but Abraham's descendants repeatedly lapsed into paganism.[17] Revival refreshing is followed by periods of prosperity and then a decline of faith. This is followed by national disaster. Then follow repentance and revival. The people forget so soon. Every generation must learn for itself all the great truths about God. No matter how well parents knew the Bible and the rich things of the good life, each generation must learn it all over again for itself. Men do not tend toward righteousness. They lean away from it. Men are born prone to sin. No man is naturally righteous. Men go astray, speaking lies as soon as they are born. They are by nature the "children of wrath." Each new generation will not learn from their elders. They must find out for themselves that sin ruins. This, by and large, is possibly the reason that men lapse into sin so quickly.

3. *The love of God.* It is impossible to read the checkered history of God's people and not be impressed with the patience and love of God. Men wilfully turn away from God and choose a path that inevitably leads to ruin. Men at the bottom of disgrace are always the objects of God's mercy. God will not let men fall eternally. God moves in, and in one way or another He rescues men. The knowledge of God is kept alive. God often calls a great prophet or preacher and endows him with a compassion for the lost

and permeates him with the Holy Spirit. Sometimes God
sends an awful judgment to punish the people and to
awaken them to their need for God and their utter de-
pendence upon Him. Then again He will permit men to
become so satiated with their own evil that they cry out
of the depths to Him. When men cry, God hears. He under-
stands the language of the soul and never fails to respond.
Out of His great love for lost men, God sends revival waves.
Faith is revived and character is redeemed. Revival is our
hope. Revival is the love of God sweeping men along like a
gentle breeze from the sea. It is the breath of God in a
Pentecostal gale. Faith will never die out of the land.[18] God
will visit and take hold of us before such a calamity prevails. One who is familiar with revivals of the Bible cannot
but expect revival.

CHAPTER 9

THE POST-CAPTIVITY REVIVAL

Nehemiah 8:1-18

The post-captivity revival came when the Persian Empire was flourishing and the Grecian Empire was fast rising to prominence. The Jews had been carried into Persia as captives. There they had made friends and had grown into great prominence and wealth. The kingdom of Persia was strong enough under Cyrus and Artaxerxes Longemanus that they had no fear of the Jews as captives and Judah as a vassal. These kings gave the Jews great liberty and favor. During the reign of Cyrus in about the year 536 B.C., a large detachment of Jews returned to Judah under the leadership of Zerubbabel and Jeshua (Ezra 1-6). Zerubbabel was assisted by the preaching of the prophets, Haggai and Zechariah. Almost seventy-five years later another expedition was led by Ezra (Ezra 7-10). Fourteen years after Ezra's expedition, Nehemiah was commissioned. He was greatly assisted by the prophet Malachi, and Ezra the scribe. Zerubbabel rebuilt the temple, and Ezra restored the law and ritual. Nehemiah, the statesman-prophet, came to restore good government and led in a much-needed reconstruction. During the days of Nehemiah's leadership, the land was visited by one of the most refreshing revivals God's people ever witnessed. Beyond every revival in the Old Testament, the post-captivity revival had the most natural setting. Every element for true revival was present. The people knew firsthand the disconcerting experience of captivity. The remnant which remained in the land had walked on thorny paths. The contingents which returned from Persia under Zerubbabel and Ezra and the remnant which had remained in the land were still continually embarrassed and tormented by scornful neighbors. The walls of Jerusalem were broken down and the city was afflicted. Despite all these afflictions, God had been with them, and for this they were very grateful. No revival comes easy. Conditions for revival will not alone nurture revival. Revival is not a spontaneous movement back to God. There is always enough opposition to thwart any such impulse. The guidance of God through yielded men is essential.

The revival really began in the distant city of Susa, the capital of Persia. It began in the heart of a young statesman when saddening news from Jerusalem reached him. A group came to the capital from Judah on an important mission to King Artaxerxes. Some of them were brethren from Jerusalem. It is not clear that any of them were more than fellow tribesmen of Judah. From the text it is not certain that any of them were blood-relations of Nehemiah. Nehemiah inquired about the status of the city. They told him that the people were sneered at, the walls of the city were destroyed, and the gates burned with fire. The people of Jerusalem were not only ridiculed, but the city was pillaged at will by marauders and vandals. Nehemiah was so concerned that he wept, fasted, and prayed before God (Neh. 1:4).

PREPARATION FOR THE REVIVAL

1. *God moved the heart of a young prophet-statesman.* Nehemiah was prepared for the challenge. He was humble. He said, "I was in Shushan" (1:1). He was reluctant to tell his real position. This is a wonderful trait for a servant of God. It is well to be slow to speak of one's own achievement. Nehemiah was rich and held a very influential position in Persia. The word "cupbearer" may mislead one. He was not the head-waiter or food-taster for King Artaxerxes. He was a very trusted person in the king's cabinet. He had learned how the Persians ruled their subjects through his close association with the king. The Persians were masters in the art of government. Apart from being schooled in

politics, he was tender and compassionate. This is an essential in a man who is to be used in a great religious awakening. He said, "I sat down and wept, and mourned certain days" (vs. 4). This does not indicate that he was soft. He was a man of decision and judgment. He was very firm and exacting, and judged fearlessly as is indicated later in the story (13:11).

2. *He was a man of prayer.* Through prayer his heart had been prepared to lead Israel in a mighty revival. Some may feel that prayer is a sign of personal weakness. But here is a wealthy, high-ranking official in the Persian empire praying like a little child before God. There is strength in prayer. In the days of the Revolutionary War the American soldiers, led by General George Washington, were suffering at Valley Forge. They were in rags and without shoes. Often they left bloodstains in the snow as they walked barefoot to do their tasks. One bleak night a soldier heard a voice ladened with prayer in the cold dark woods. He drew nearer and recognized the voice as that of General Washington praying for his men.[1] Great men pray as they struggle against the vicissitudes of life.

Nehemiah said two vital things in his prayer. First, he confessed the sins of Israel and his own sins. He admitted that he and his father's house had dealt corruptly with God and had not kept the commandments nor the statutes which God had commanded Moses (1:6-7). Nehemiah knew one thing that every person must learn; he knew that God could not bless him over unconfessed sins. If there is a sin in one's life, it must be given up or the blessings of God can never get through. Sin blocks the flow of God's blessings. A man may be in the middle of the sea of God's grace but not one drop of it can get in if any sin corks up the entrance.[2] Every man who ever received the benefits of God had to confess his sins. This is where Hezekiah, as well as David and Daniel, began. There have been no exceptions to the rule.

In the second place, Nehemiah reminded Jehovah of His promises. "Remember, I beseech thee, the word that

thou commandedst thy servant Moses, saying, If ye trans-
gress, I will scatter you abroad among the nations: But if
ye turn unto me, and keep my commandments, and do
them; though there were of you cast out unto the uttermost
part of the heaven, yet will I gather them from thence, and
will bring them unto the place that I have chosen to set my
name there" (vss. 8-9). The young stateman reminded
God that though the people had been scattered because of
their sins, now they had returned to the statutes of God, and
were expecting His blessings. The prayer of Nehemiah was
strong and persistent. He did not hit and run in his peti-
tions. He prayed two months and no answer came. Then
he prayed two more months. For four months he prayed
to his God before the slightest signs of an answer came.
He prayed from December until April (1:1; 2:1). Then the
answer came like a cloudburst. Within a few minutes from
the first sign of an answer, he had the full answer in his
hands. That is the way prayer works.

Conditions must be right and hearts must be prepared
to hold God's prayer answers. This may be why He often
delays His answers. God needed an instrument with which
to perform the answer to Nehemiah's prayer. Nehemiah
was the instrument, but he had to be willing to yield. It is
a dangerous thing to pray for a great cause unless you mean
it. When Nehemiah first began to pray, he prayed for God
to gather and bless the troubled people in Jerusalem. After
four months of prayer he could say, "Send me unto Judah"
(2:5). If a man prays earnestly and persistently unto God,
he may find that God will use only him to answer the
prayer. If one prays earnestly enough for a pioneer area
or for the Middle East or Hong Kong, he may find it necessary to answer God's promptings to labor there. If one prays
for a revival and really means it, he may find it necessary
to make certain surrenders and pay the price to be the instrument God would use to help bring the revival.

It meant a great deal to give up his place in the palace
at Susa.[3] He held a lofty position and had plenty of money
and much luxury. He gave all this up for the rigors of lead-

ing a defeated and discouraged people back to God and national strength. He renounced a life of ease and luxury and political advancement for a life of toil and heartbreak. In this respect he approximates Moses who could have been the Pharaoh of Egypt, but chose instead to suffer hardships and peril with the children of Israel. It seems that Moses and Nehemiah preferred the will of God to any other advantage on earth. This is a difficult lesson to learn. Only recently a pastor in one of our great southern churches would have chosen only the pastorate for himself. For almost ten years God endeavored to call him to full-time evangelism. He loved the security of his pastorate and cherished the love of the people, but finally he decided to cease to be the trustee of his own life and let God take complete charge. These have been the most glorious ten years of his life. There is no experience comparable to being in the dead center of God's will.

Prayer changes a man's heart and alters his outlook. But it does more; it even changes his facial expressions. When Nehemiah came before Artaxerxes, the king could see the change in facial expression and asked, "Why is thy countenance sad, seeing thou are not sick? (2:2). Nehemiah was burdened but not really sad; but concern was reflected in his face. It was more than a burdened look. It was a stamp of heaven. The pagan king could detect the radical change but could not describe it. Nehemiah told the king the plight of his people in Judah, and the king asked, "For what dost thou make request?" His answer was immediately forthcoming but not until he sent up one more brief pointed prayer to God, "So I prayed to the God of heaven." He no doubt asked God to help him phrase his request. He knew that beautiful words would not suffice. He needed the touch of God. He asked for it and received it, for his request found favor with the king. Soon he was preparing to travel to Jerusalem to rebuild the walls and to lead in the most remarkable period of reconstruction ever known in the history of the Jewish people.

3. *Nehemiah in Jerusalem.* The king's cabinet member

was in Jerusalem three days before he began his work (2:11-12). The citizens had no idea why this high-ranking officer from Susa, the capital, had arrived in their dilapidated city. It is very likely that neither Ezra nor Malachi knew the purpose of Nehemiah's visit. Nehemiah did not employ fanfare nor did he care for the shouts of empty praise. If the city had known why he had come, they would have rolled out the royal carpet and shouted themselves hoarse. It is better to wait to celebrate until the work is done.

At the outset, Nehemiah did four things in Jerusalem. All of these acts combined to lay the foundation for revival.

(1) He surveyed the city. He viewed the ruins (vss. 12-16). He found a worse condition than had been reported. The magnitude of the task would have chilled the fervor of a merely ambitious man. It challenged a man, however, with great character and a purpose. He had not come to Jerusalem looking for an easy job. And he was not discouraged when he faced the stupendous task. He might have remained in Susa with ease, plenty, and the glory of dazzling thrones and marble floors. But if he had, he never would have been heard of. He answered a challenge and went at all hazards where he was needed. His name lives in the neon signs of Holy Scripture forever.

(2) He challenged Jerusalem. "Let us build up the walls of Jerusalem that we be no more a reproach." They were encouraged by his words. He said, "Let us build." He also added, "that we be no more a reproach." He identified himself with them. This was unexpected and at first shocked them. Then it inspired them to undertake the impossible. If a nobleman from the courts in Shushan was one of them, and if he would roll up his sleeves and work with them, they would build. Jubilation filled the city. They were ready to follow him. If one reads the history of these people, he will be in position to understand their preparedness to answer such a challenge. Some seventy years before this, fifty thousand of these people or their parents had returned from Persia with great joy (Ezra 2:64-65). For five months or more they had marched through hardships. When they

arrived in Jerusalem, they went to work to build the temple. Zerubbabel led them to give sacrificially. They had willingly given over four hundred thousand dollars to build the temple (Ezra 2:69). A poor, distressed, poverty-stricken group of slaves could not have given such a magnificent offering if they had not been possessed of great love and dedication. With sheer determination they built Zerubbabel's temple. No house in history ever matched the glory and splendor of Solomon's temple, yet greater glory was to come to this house than to Solomon's temple. In this very temple Jesus worshiped four hundred years later. These very stones which Zerubbabel handled stood intact to see the day of the Lord on earth.

(3) The walls of Jerusalem were rebuilt. The walls were rebuilt despite opposition from without and misgivings from within. The devil never fails to use opposition when God's people rise up to build; the devil always attacks. There is no case in history where this has not been true. Even in the building of a new addition to the church this is true. Two things guaranteed the building of the walls. The people were thoroughly organized, and they had a mind to work. They were well organized. Eliashib the high priest and his brethren built the sheep-gate, and the large towers on either side (Neh. 3:1). "Next unto him builded the men of Jericho" and the space of the wall "next to them builded Zaccur the son of Imri" (3:2), and on and on until every foot of the wall was assigned, and the men set in to build each his share. Many well-meaning people decry organization in the work of God. Those who oppose organization, however, are either ignorant of the Bible or they show lack of ingenuity. "The people had a mind to work" (4:6). God's people can accomplish unbelievable feats under strenuous circumstances if they are dedicated to it. The parents of these people had built the temple under ridicule and political intrigue, and now their children were building the walls of the city because they had made up their minds not to be detoured.

(4) Formidable opposition was met with prayer,

wisdom, and undivided allegiance. Ridicule from Samaria
and the Amorites could not stop them from without. Then
the enemy tried to work from within the city. They circulated stories among the inhabitants of the city saying that
they, would come in unawares and slay the people. Discouraged brethren inside the camp can do more to stop the
work of God than all the opposition from the outside. San-
ballat, Tobiah, and Geshem tried stratagem by urging Nehemiah to come out on the plains of Ono and work out a
peaceful co-existence. Nehemiah replied, "I am doing a
great work, so that I cannot come down" (6:3). Many a
reformer and builder has buried his dreams on the plains of
Ono. There is never any profit to God's people by collusion
with the enemy.

PERFORMANCE IN THE REVIVAL

The walls were built within fifty-two days. As soon as
the walls were completed, the people were registered and
the remnant was numbered. Hope had been born, and the
spirit of the people was healthy and bright. Nehemiah had
not finished his work. Strong walls of protection and a
bright spirit are not enough to build a nation. They needed
a deeper spiritual life. This was within the plan of the great
leader. Nehemiah sanctioned and promoted the revival, but
Ezra actually led the people in the performance.

1. *The people were assembled in the street just inside
the water gate.* This gate was at the east end of the city
close to the temple, a part of the sacred enclosure. The
gathering took place on the day of the feast of the trumpets
(Num. 29:1), which is October 1. It was an ideal day for
a great religious gathering for it was a day of holy convocation. It was also on this day that they had made burnt
offerings on their return from captivity. The feast of trumpets was a time of testimony. Being a holy day was not as
important, however, as what transpired at the gathering in
the open air.

The scene which took place is unique in history. Ezra
stood on a large wooden pulpit where all the people in the

great assembly could see him. Thirteen priests stood on the
platform with him, six on the left hand, and seven on the
right.[4] At the request of the people Ezra brought the scroll
of the law and held it in his hand in full view. With hungry
eyes the expectant crowd looked upon the book. "When
he [Ezra] opened it, all the people stood up (8:5). He read
from the book from early morning until midday (vs. 3). He
did not read continuously. He would read a section and
then the Levites would repair to their respective places
among the great congregation and "cause the people to
understand the law" (vs. 7).[5] They "gave the sense" (vs. 8)
means that they expounded the meaning of the Scripture
to them. The book of the law was not a spring of living
water to be sealed off or a treasure to be locked up. It was
a lamp to the path and food to the soul. It was to be
brought out in reach of the people. The reading of the
Word by Ezra blessed their hearts, but the exposition of it
by the Levites fed them with the bread of life. "The people
stood in their places" means that several of the Levites were
in different places in the congregation expounding the Scriptures simultaneously.

The main method was the distinct reading from the
book of the law. They were hungry to hear the detailed
instructions of the law. The multiplex precepts of the law
were recited and explained to the men, women, and little
children. The most sacred rites, in all their intricate details,
were read to the assembly. Much of the law was occupied
with directions to the priests concerning the function of
ritual, but the ordinary laymen needed to have some idea
of it. Such instructions would safeguard against sacerdotal-
ism.[6] It is likely however that most of the reading came
from certain sections of Deuteronomy which were adapted
to convict the people. The people gave rapt attention to
the reading and bowed and worshiped God in an attitude of
reverence (vs. 6).

The first two days of the open-air assembly was moral
and not ceremonial in nature. It was an assembly of prayer,
Bible reading, and preaching. Ceremonies were employed

later in the week. But the first assemblies were strictly moral in method and tone. The people were convicted of sin, and they repented when they heard the law. "All the people wept" (vs. 9). To weep is not always a sign of true repentance but in this case there is no doubt that repentance was genuine. The law revealed their sins to them. It showed them the danger of sin. When they heard from the law how they had sinned, exposed themselves, and offended God, it greatly moved them. They recognized their guilt before God. Until men recognize their guilt, there can be no repentance. And without repentance there can be no reconciliation with God. Without repentance and forgiveness there can be no revival. When the law was expounded to them, they repented with a godly sorrow; and the revival was on.

When Nehemiah and Ezra and the Levites who assisted them saw the people weep, they urged them to "mourn not . . . for this day is a holy day unto our LORD . . . for the joy of the LORD is your strength" (vss. 9-10). With great difficulty they quieted the people. The Levites continued to console the repentant for long hours after the speech of Ezra and the governor (vs. 11). To weep was a good sign and the leaders understood why they wept. Weeping prepared the way for joyous celebration. The purpose of sorrow for guilt is that one may receive the joy God administers in forgiveness. True repentance with biblical instructions produces a lasting joy. Those who really rejoice in the Lord cannot help but share their joy. It cannot be kept. They had a sharing religion. They sent "portions unto them for whom nothing is prepared" (vs. 10). This means that they sent part of their good food and sweet drinks to the poor that they might join in the joyous celebration. There is no place in revealed religion for selfishness. We share our joys and our bounties with those about us. God does not bless one man with more money than another because he esteems that man above another. God often overruns the storehouse of one man that He in turn may help the needy in the name of Christ and thereby magnify the name of Jehovah in the earth.

2. *On the second day a twofold assembly was held.* The first part of the assembly was attended by "the chief of the fathers of all the people, the priests, and the Levites" (vs. 13). They came unto Ezra the scribe for instructions that they might better "understand the words of the law" (vs. 13). On the first day, in humility, Ezra asked the religious leaders to sit on the platform with him. On the second day their humility set them at his feet. They had tried to assist the first day by expounding the law. They realized that to do it effectively they needed instructions. This was the purpose for the assembly, of the chiefs of the people, and of the Levites early on the second day. They learned from searching the law under Ezra that when they had formerly observed the Feast of the Tabernacles, they had failed to observe the precept concerning the booths. They prepared to celebrate the approaching festival according to the instructions of the law (Lev. 23:39-43). The rest of the second day was spent in reading the law to the whole congregation, and in the observance of various offerings which were specified in Leviticus (Lev. 23:33-38). For seven days they offered offerings made by fire. These offerings consisted of burnt offerings, thank offerings, etc.

3. *The Feast of the Tabernacles restored.* On the fifteenth day of October they began observing the Feast of the Tabernacles. Each family took boughs of myrtle, olive, palms and other thick-boughed trees and made booths. They dwelt in them for seven days. Some constructed the booths on their lawns, some on the top of their homes, and some in the open spaces in the streets. The people who had gathered from other villages and cities erected their booths in the streets and near the temple. This was the first time that this particular precept had been observed by the whole community in over a thousand years (vs. 17). It commemorated the time when they dwelt in booths as God brought them up out of Egypt. Each day the book of the law was read, and on the eighth day a solemn assembly was called.

"And there was very great gladness" (vs. 17). Just as very great sorrow had characterized the people on the first day of the Feast of the Trumpets, so great gladness characterized them at the end of the Feast of the Tabernacles. This was a joy that sprang up in their hearts by means of their relation to God. It was a God-given gladness and was found in sweet fellowship with God. God-given gladness is as far above mere human gladness as the righteousness of God is above the righteousness of men. The source of this gladness was God. He was glad at the repentance and performance of the people, and the gladness became a contagion, spreading from the heart of God to the people. This kind of gladness is too wonderful for words and can never be known except by people in communion with God. The service of Baal was a terror. It was agony and fear to his most loyal devotees. The heart of God is reflected in the worshiper. The heart of God is filled with indescribable beauty, love, and happiness. When the people in Jerusalem got close to Him in fellowship, these wonderful traits of God were reflected in their hearts.

4. *On the twenty-fourth day of the month of October, only two days after the Feast of the Tabernacles, they reassembled in the temple.* There they (1) humbled themselves by mourning and fasting; (2) listened to the reading of the law; and (3) "confessed their sins, and iniquities of their fathers" (9:2). The book of the law was read for three hours each day and then another three-hour period was spent in confession. (4) The priests and Levites directed them in praising God (9:4-5). It is likely that the priests and Levites sang a liturgical hymn, and the congregation responded in a chorus of praise. The praise was followed by a prayer of confession (9:6-38). It seems to be the prayer of the whole congregation. Revival was in full bloom, for the people had humbled themselves in sackcloth and heaped dirt upon their heads. They had confessed the sins of their elders and their own sins, and now the whole temple rang with hymns of praise and prayers of confession and gratitude. It was a great and memorable day. The

whole effort seemed to climax on the twenty-fourth day of
October. The following weeks and months, however, would
declare the depths of the meeting, as well as its lasting
effects.

EFFECTS OF THE REVIVAL

1. *The post-captivity revival was, in many respects, the
most far-reaching revival recorded in the Old Testament.* It
abolished idolatry forever among the Jews. We have no
record that as a people they ever lapsed into idolatry after
the post-captivity revival. They became so suspicious against
anything that smacked of foreign religions and differed
from the law of Moses that Jesus and the disciples four
hundred years later met with stubborn resistance.

2. *It issued in the rectifying of many wrong relations.*[7]
The Israelites separated themselves from the Moabites and
Amorites. They discontinued mixed congregations (13:1,
3). They discontinued mixed marriages (13:23-31). Many
of the Jews had married wives of Ashdod and Moab, and
their children spoke foreign languages. Nehemiah contended
with them about the matter until they decided to refuse to
let their sons and daughters intermarry with pagans. He
used the power of the revival to help curb this dangerous
practice. If he had tried to rectify this evil when he first
arrived in Jerusalem, they would not have listened to him.
But when the power of revival came and hearts were
changed, most of them were open to instructions. The principles of ethics are powerless by themselves. Revival fires
must etch them into the consciences of men. Preachments
about duty fall to the ground when they are not animated
by deep convictions.

3. *They determined to maintain public worship in the
house of God.* They were determined never to let go the
benefits which they had recently received in the holy convocations.

4. *They reinstituted the tithe* (13:11-12). It was vital
that the priests and Levites give full time to the services of
God's house. The tithe had not been given and the Levites
were forced to work in the fields, thereby neglecting the

house of God (13:10-11). Nehemiah gathered them together and set them in their place. "Then brought all Judah
the tithe" (13:12). Malachi had preached very strongly the
necessity of the tithe, and with the help of the governor
and the momentum of the revival, it was once again put
into practice (Mal. 3:8-11).

5. *Sabbath observance was restored* (13:15-26). Nehemiah observed the people bringing in grapes and figs and all
kinds of burdens for sale on the Sabbath. He warned them
to discontinue sales of victuals on the Sabbath. Along with
the local merchants, cattlemen, and farmers, came men from
Tyre to sell fish and all kinds of ware on the Sabbath.
Nehemiah rebuked the citizens of Jerusalem for the pro-
fanation of the holy day. When his warnings and speeches
availed little, he took strong measures by closing the gates
of Jerusalem on the Sabbath and shutting out the salesmen.
When they camped around the walls and bootlegged victuals to the inhabitants, Nehemiah ordered them away and
threatened them with force. He succeeded in breaking it
up in two ways: by closing the gates of the city on the
Sabbath, and by providing worship in the temple for the
people. He commanded the Levites to serve in the temple
on the Sabbath. The wise leader knew full well that a
negative emphasis must be bolstered with positive measures.

NOTES

REVIVAL

CHAPTER 1

1. W. E. Biederwolf, *Evangelism* (New York: Fleming H. Revell Co., 1921), p. 19.
2. James Burns, *Revivals, Their Laws and Leaders* (London: Hodder & Stoughton, 1949), p. 3.
3. *Ibid.*, p. 19.
4. A. B. Strickland, *The Great American Revival* (Cincinnati: Standard Press, 1934), p. 23.
5. *Burns, op. cit.*, p. 3.
6. *Ibid.*, p. 4.
7. *Ibid.*, p. 6.
8. Charles G. Finney, *Revival Lectures* (London: Fleming H. Revell Company, n.d.), p. 4.
9. Biederwolf, *op. cit.*, p. 19.
10. John Shearer, *Old Time Revivals* (Fort Worth: Potter's Book Store, 1958), p. 40.
11. B. R. Lacy, Jr., *Revivals in the Midst of the Years* (Richmond: John Knox Press, 1943), p. 11.
12. Burns, *op. cit.*, p. 10.
13. Oswald J. Smith, *The Revival We Need* (London: Marshall, Morgan & Scott, Ltd., 1933), p. 47.
14. *Ibid.*, p. 48.
15. W. L. Muncy, Jr., *A History of Evangelism in the United States* (Kansas City: Central Seminary Press, 1945), p. 60.
16. *Ibid.*, p. 61.
17. Warren A. Candler, *Great Revivals and the Great Republic* (Nashville: The Publishing House of the Methodist Church, South, 1924), p. 27.
18. Lacy, *op. cit.*, p. 12.
19. Roland Q. Leavell, *Evangelism, Christ's Imperative Commission* (Nashville: Broadman Press, 1951), pp. 57-58.
20. Strickland, *op. cit.*, p. 45.
21. John S. Simon, *The Revival of Religion in England in the Eighteenth Century* (London: Charles H. Kelly), pp. 96-98.
22. Muncy, *op. cit.*, p. 26.

23. *Ibid.*, p. 24.
24. Simon, *op. cit.*, p. 122.
25. Raymond Calkins, *How Jesus Dealt with Men* (New York: Abingdon-Cokesbury Press, 1942), p. 40.
26. Alfred M. Perry, *The Interpreter's Bible*, Vol. 7 (New York: Abingdon Press, 1951), p. 69.
27. *Ibid.*, p. 69.
28. *Ibid.*, p. 69.
29. *Ibid.*, p. 70.
30. *Ibid.*, p. 70.

THE REVIVAL AT SINAI

Chapter 2

1. George Rawlinson, *The Pulpit Commentary* (Chicago: Wilcox and Follett Company, n.d.), p. 323.
2. J. P. Lange, *Commentary on Holy Scriptures* (Exodus) (New York: Charles Scribner & Sons, 1876), p. 134.
3. E. D. Head, *Revivals in the Bible* (Unpublished lecture notes), p. 2.
4. Rawlinson, *op. cit.*, p. 348.
5. *Ibid.*, p. 349.
6. *Ibid.*, p. 349.
7. Lange, *op. cit.*, p. 138.
8. Alfred M. Perry, *The Interpreter's Bible* (New York: Abingdon Press, 1952), Vol. 1, p. 1072.
9. Head, *op. cit.*, p. 2.
10. Matthew Henry, *Commentary on the Whole Bible* (New York: Fleming H. Revell Co., 1708), Vol. 1, Exodus 33:4.
11. S. R. Driver, *The Cambridge Bible* (*Exodus*) (Cambridge: University Press, 1911), p. 358.
12. C. F. Keil and F. Delitzsch, *The Pentateuch* (Grand Rapids: Eerdmans Publishing Co., 1949), Vol. 2, p. 235.
13. *Ibid*, p. 236.

THE REVIVAL UNDER SAMUEL

Chapter 3

1. A. F. Kirkpatrick, *The Cambridge Bible* (*I Samuel*) (Cambridge: The University Press, 1899). p. 80.
2. *Ibid.*, p. 85.
3. *Ibid.*, p. 85.
4. Alexander Maclaren, *Expositions of Holy Scripture* (Grand Rapids: Eerdmans Publishing Company, 1944), Vol. 2, p. 284.
5. Kirkpatrick, *op. cit.*, p. 87.
6. *Ibid.*, p. 88.

7. J. B. Cranfill, *From Nature to Grace* (Nashville: The Sunday School Board, 1924), p. 118.
8. W. Robertson Nicoll, *The Expositor's Bible* (Grand Rapids: Eerdmans Publishing Company, 1940), Vol. 2, p. 29.
9. Kirkpatrick, *op. cit.,* p. 91.
10. Maclaren, *op. cit.,* p. 290.

THE REVIVAL ON MOUNT CARMEL

CHAPTER 4

1. W. Milligan, *Elijah, His Life and Times* (New York: Fleming H. Revell Company, n.d.), p. 4.
2. G. H. Fraser, *Elijah the Pilgrim Prophet* (Chicago: Moody Press, 1956), p. 21.
3. J. R. Macduff, *Elijah, the Prophet of Fire* (Grand Rapids: Baker Book House, 1956), p. 21.
4. Fraser, *op. cit.,* p. 24.
5. F. W. Krummacher, *Elijah the Tishbite* (Grand Rapids: Zondervan Publishing House, n.d.), p. 7.
6. Arthur W. Pink, *The Life of Elijah* (Grand Rapids: Zondervan Publishing House, 1956), p. 19.
7. W. M. Taylor, *Elijah the Prophet* (New York: Harper & Brothers, 1875), p. 14.
8. H. T. Howat, *Elijah the Desert Prophet* (Edinburgh: Johnstone, Hunter & Co., 1868), p. 22.
9. Pink, *op. cit.,* p. 118.
10. Taylor, *op. cit.,* p. 69.
11. R. G. Macintyre, *Elijah and Elisha* (Edinburgh: T. & T. Clark, n.d.), p. 22.

THE REVIVAL AT NINEVEH

CHAPTER 5

1. H. C. O. Lanchester, *The Cambridge Bible* (Cambridge: University Press, 1918), p. 65.
2. C. F. Keil, *Biblical Commentary on the Old Testament* (Grand Rapids: Eerdmans Publishing Co., 1949), p. 390.
3. John Urquhart, *The New Biblical Guide* (Chicago: W. P. Blessing, n.d.), Vol. 7, p. 141.
4. Lanchester, *op. cit.,* p. 52.
5. William Smith, *A Dictionary of the Bible* (Philadelphia: John C. Winston Co., 1884), p. 449.
6. Lanchester, *op. cit.,* p. 71.
7. James Hardee Kennedy, *Studies in the Book of Jonah* (Nashville: Broadman Press, 1956), p. 4.

8. Keil, *op. cit.*, p. 384.
9. *Ibid.*, p. 393.
10. Kennedy, *op. cit.*, p. 35.
11. Keil, *op. cit.*, p. 399.
12. George Adam Smith, *The Book of the Twelve Prophets* (London: Hodder and Stoughton, 1929), p. 495.
13. *Ibid.*, p. 495.
14. Kennedy, *op. cit.*, p. 51.
15. Keil, *op. cit.*, p. 409.

THE REVIVAL UNDER ASA

CHAPTER 6

1. Ernest Baker, *The Revivals of the Bible* (London: The Kingsgate Press, 1906), p. 37.
2. William Winston, *Genuine Works of Josephus* (Chicago: Thompson and Thompson, n.d.), p. 413.
3. Baker, *op. cit.*, p. 40.
4. *Ibid.*, p. 46.
5. W. H. Bennett, *Expositor's Bible* (Grand Rapids: Eerdmans Publishing Co., 1940), Vol. 2, p. 555.
6. *Ibid.*, p. 556.
7. W. A. L. Elmslie, *The Interpreter's Bible* (Nashville: Abingdon Press, 1954), Vol. 3, p. 484.
8. C. F. Keil, *The Biblical Commentary* (Edinburgh: T. & T. Clark, 1872), p. 369.
9. W. A. L. Elmslie, *The Cambridge Bible* (Cambridge: University Press, 1916), p. 235.

THE REVIVAL LED BY HEZEKIAH

CHAPTER 7

1. Matthew Henry, *Commentary on the Whole Bible* (New York: Fleming H. Revell Co., 1708), Vol. II, II Chronicles 29, Section III.
2. H. C. O. Lanchester, *The Cambridge Bible* (Cambridge: University Press, 1899), p. 256.
3. Wilbur M. Smith, *The Glorious Revival under King Hezekiah* (Grand Rapids: Zondervan Publishing House, 1954), p. 36.
4. Lanchester, *op. cit.*, p. 256.
5. Alexander Maclaren, *Expositions of Holy Scripture* (Grand Rapids: Eerdmans Publishing Co., 1944), Vol. 3, p. 236.
6. Ernest Baker, *The Revivals of the Bible* (London: Kingsgage Press, 1906), p. 69.

7. Smith, *op. cit.*, p. 37.
8. *Ibid.*, p. 38.
9. *Ibid.*, p. 41.

THE REVIVAL UNDER JOSIAH

Chapter 8

1. W. A. L. Elmslie, *The Interpreter's Bible* (Nashville: Abingdon Press, 1954), Vol. 3, p. 536.
2. Ernest Baker, *The Revivals of the Bible* (London: Kingsgate Press, 1906), p. 82.
3. *Ibid.*, p. 76.
4. Alexander Maclaren, *Expositions of Holy Scripture* (Grand Rapids: Eerdmans Publishing Co., 1944), Vol. 3, p. 259.
5. Cunningham Geikie, *Hours with the Bible* (London: Hodder & Stoughton, 1882), p. 217.
6. *Ibid.*, p. 217.
7. W. A. L. Elmslie, *The Cambridge Bible* (Cambridge: University Press, 1916), p. 338.
8. Geikie, *op. cit.*, p. 221.
9. *Ibid.*, p. 221.
10. *Ibid.*, p. 221.
11. *Ibid.*, p. 225.
12. Maclaren, *op. cit.*, p. 263.
13. Baker, *op cit.*, p. 82.
14. J. B. Lawrence, *Kindling for Revival Fires* (London: Fleming H. Revell Co., 1940), p. 18.
15. Elmslie, *The Interpreter's Bible,* p. 541.
16. Geikie, *op. cit.*, p. 254.
17. Baker, *op. cit.*, p. 79.
18. *Ibid.*, p. 81.

THE POST-CAPTIVITY REVIVAL

Chapter 9

1. J. B. Cranfill, *From Nature to Grace* (Nashville: Sunday School Board, 1924), p. 174.
2. D. L. Moody, *Men of the Bible* (Chicago: Fleming H. Revell Co., 1898), p. 55.
3. *Ibid.*, p. 59.
4. C. F. Keil, *Biblical Commentary on the Old Testament* (Grand Rapids: Eerdmans Publishing Co., 1950), p. 229.
5. W. Robertson Nicoll, *The Expositor's Bible* (Grand Rapids: Eerdmans Publishing Co., 1940), Vol. 2, p. 656.
6. *Ibid.*, p. 657.
7. Ernest Baker, *The Revivals of the Bible* (London: Kingsgage Press, 1904), p. 122.